Writing a thesis

a guide to long essays and
dissertations

George Watson

Longman
London and New York

Longman Group UK Limited
Longman House, Burnt Mill, Harlow
Essex CM20 2JE, England
and Associated Companies throughout the world

*Published in the United States of America
by Longman Inc., New York*

First published 1987
Seventh impression 1993

British Library Cataloguing in Publication Data
Watson, George, 1927–
    Writing a thesis : a quick guide to long essays
    and dissertations.
    1. Dissertations, Academic
    I. Title
    808'.02   LB 2369
    ISBN 0-582-49465-6

Library of Congress Cataloging in Publication Data
Watson, George, 1927–
    Writing a thesis,

    Bibliography: p.
    Includes index.
    1. Report writing.   2. Research.   3. Dissertations,
Academic.   I. Title.
LB2369.W34   1987   808'.02   86–2818
ISBN 0-582-49465-6 (pbk.)

Set in 10/12pt Linotron 202 Bembo
Printed in Malaysia by TCP

Contents

Preface

Writing a thesis used to be something for those experienced in scholarship – or at least something for graduates.

No longer. In the past twenty years it has become a common part of the preparation for a first degree; and the extended essay can even be part of ordinary usage in upper forms at schools. That new urge is the occasion for this book, which is meant for graduates and undergraduates alike, and even for those not yet entered into higher education at all. 'The power of instruction is seldom of much efficacy,' wrote Gibbon in the *Decline and Fall*, 'except in those happy dispositions where it is almost superfluous' (ch. 4). But I cannot think this book superfluous. No one ever wrote a thesis by the light of nature; and those who imagine that being intelligent and having something to say are enough have been known to fall flat on their faces when they try. With better warnings, or closer attention to warnings, they might have fared better. A thesis is not a dash for freedom: it can be an entry into an entirely unfamiliar world of restraint, and not all beginners understand that by its nature it is a more confining exercise than answering a three-hour paper in an examination room. A thesis needs to be rigorously shaped, for one thing; for another, it needs to be efficiently documented; and though a question written under examination-conditions is always the better for being shaped, no one expects it to be documented in a scholarly sense. Writing a thesis is not a self-liberating choice, then. It is more like learning a game with new rules.

This book is about how to write scholarly prose, how to shape it, and how to document it. It is meant to stimulate literary and historical research on the one hand, and help towards disciplining it on the other; and if students of law, economics and the sciences can find profit in its advice, so much the better. It is based on the assumption that a thesis is not a kind of essay – certainly not an over-grown essay – and that those imagine that an ability to write good essays has prepared them to write a thesis are inviting disappoint-ment. A thesis is a radically different activity: more severely argued, more consistently documented, and more rigorously shaped and lucidly segmented. It cannot afford the loose style or arrangement of an essay: at least not beyond its first draft. It is something else. There is a quantum leap between the two forms, and this book exists to help the student to measure the effort that will be required of him and to train his mind to an unaccustomed task. This is a book for beginners – but for beginners who want to go on.

It begins with some general considerations and narrows as it continues, holding technicality at bay for as long as it can and segregating issues as severely as the nature of the argument allows. There is a well-known dilemma here which the book illustrates as well as debates: to omit the larger theoretical issues is to invite an easy objection that one is indifferent to the most vexed intellectual issues of the age; to discuss them is to attract the opposite complaint that sensible people are no longer interested in the fading theoretical fervours of the 1960s. I have tried to meet both these objections, contradictory as they are, by beginning the book with chapters devoted to some of the wider motives of scholarship and its more momentous hopes and fears – Part One: 'The approach' – followed by a second part entitled 'The techniques', where more specific problems are signposted by explanatory titles. No need, then, to assume that the book is best read in the order in which it is presented. It is one of the most essential arts of scholarship to learn how to quarry a book efficiently for what one wants to learn from it; and some chapters here, such as 'The lure of theory' or 'Editing a text', can be sidestepped by anyone incurious about critical theory or indifferent to the charms of editorship.

Some of these remarks began as lectures to undergraduates reading English at Cambridge or to graduate students in English and Modern Languages there, and they have profited in all sorts of ways from their earnest and sceptical attention. Disagreement is the live-liest form of flattery, as they knew, and the only useful form; and close attention is not to be confused with assent. It is out of their attention and disagreement that this book has grown and flourished, and I dedicate it in gratitude to my Cambridge pupils. And my thanks are due also to Renford Bambrough and Christopher Ricks, for letting me share their seminars and their advice.

St John's College, Cambridge   G. W.
October 1985

PART ONE
The approach

An equal expression of what the world knows and what the world
does not know will not be read by the world.

Walter Bagehot

CHAPTER ONE
Why scholars write

Whatever may be the present extent of human knowledge, it is not only finite, and therefore in its own nature capable of increase; but so narrow, that almost every understanding may by a diligent application of its powers hope to enlarge it.

It is, however, not necessary that a man should forbear to write, till he has discovered some truth unknown before; he may be sufficiently useful by only diversifying the surface of knowledge, and luring the mind by a new appearance to a second view of those beauties which it had passed over inattentively before. Every writer may find intellects correspondent to his own, to whom his expressions are familiar, and his thoughts congenial; and perhaps truth is often more successfully propagated by men of moderate abilities who, adopting the opinions of others, have no care but to explain them clearly, than by subtile speculatists and curious searchers, who exact from their readers powers equal to their own, and if their fabrics of science be strong take no care to render them accessible . . .

If we apply to authors themselves for an account of their state, it will appear very little to deserve envy; for they have in all ages been addicted to complaint. The neglect of learning, the ingratitude of the present age, and the absurd preference by which ignorance and dullness often obtain favour and rewards, have been from age to age topics of invective; and few have left their names to posterity, without some appeal to future candour from the perverseness and malice of their own times.

I have, nevertheless, been often inclined to doubt whether authors, however querulous, are in reality more miserable than their fellow mortals. The present life is to all a state of infelicity; every man, like any author, believes himself to merit more than he obtains, and solaces the present with the prospect of the future: others, indeed, suffer those disappointments in silence of which the writer complains, to shew how well he has learnt the art of lamentation . . .

It frequently happens that a design which, when considered at a distance, gave flattering hopes of facility, mocks us in the execution with unexpected difficulties; the mind which, while it considered it in the gross, imagined itself amply furnished with materials, finds sometimes an unexpected barrenness and vacuity, and wonders whither all those ideas are vanished, which a little before seemed struggling for emission.

Sometimes many thoughts present themselves; but so confused and unconnected that they are not without difficulty reduced to method, or concatenated in a regular and dependent series: the mind falls at once into a labyrinth of which neither the beginning nor end can be discovered, and toils and struggles without progress or extrication . . .

It is one of the common distresses of a writer to be within a word of a happy period, to want only a single epithet to give amplification its full force, to require only a correspondent term in order to finish a paragraph with elegance and make one of its members answer to the other: but these deficiencies cannot always be supplied; and after long study and vexation, the passage is turned anew, and the web unwoven that was nearly finished.

But when thoughts and words are collected and adjusted, and the whole composition at last concluded, it seldom gratifies the author, when he comes coolly and deliberately to review it, with the hopes which had been excited in the fury of the performance: novelty always captivates the mind; as our thoughts rise fresh upon us, we readily believe them just and original, which, when the pleasure of production is over, we find to be mean and common, or borrowed from the works of others, and supplied by memory rather than invention.

But though it should happen that the writer finds no such faults in his performance, he is still to remember that he looks upon it with partial eyes; and when he considers how much men who could judge of others with great exactness have often failed in judging of themselves, he will be afraid of deciding too hastily in his own favour, or of allowing himself to contemplate with too much complacence treasure that has not yet been brought to the test, nor passed the only trial that can stamp its value.

Samuel Johnson, *The Adventurer* nos 137–8 (February–March 1754)

A thesis is a first attempt to be a scholar.

Why, then, do scholars write? The answer, which is not always entirely obvious to a beginner, is to declare a discovery that the world needs and will take note of – usually by publishing it. The scholar declares a discovery the world has some use for. His activity is not merely decorative, that is to say, or self-educative – even though the thesis is nowadays rightly seen as a prime educative device. Nor is what he writes to be judged by its sincerity, since a view can be thoroughly sincere and thoroughly useless. Unlike a student essay, a thesis exists *for others*. In intention, at least, it is to be used by somebody else. If it succeeds, it will have an existence beyond the interests of its author: and some one will be grateful for it who knows and cares nothing of its author.

It is here at the start, and before the topic is chosen, that the thesis diverges from the student essay, or from class-teaching and ordinary literary and historical conversation. It exists, or tries to exist, in its own right. It is not an expression of personal enthusiasm, however much its origins may lie there; and it is not, at least in its purpose, self-revelatory. It is the product of a workshop, not of a playground. Even if it is never published, it ought (ideally speaking) to be publishable, at least in part; and even if in the event it is not publishable, it ought at least to look as if it is trying to be that. It seeks and welcomes the discipline of other minds.

That discipline is bracing as well as humbling, and scholars – even as beginners – necessarily write in some awareness of other minds. They expect, even crave, the criticism of others. To be criticized, after all, however sternly, is to be noticed; and to be noticed, in that world, is to succeed. A thesis asks to be criticized, and it is built with a view to stand criticism much as a ship is built for the open sea. What scholars properly and rationally fear is not criticism but neglect: that what they write will be seen as so obscure, so trivial, or so trite, that no one will criticize it at all.

The scholar writes, then, to attract attention to a view. He cannot, like the author of a student essay, reasonably expect any interest in himself as a person, in the first instance, and it is wise to assume no such thing. An essay or student paper can be written for a captive audience – often an audience of one. A thesis, by contrast, is a first attempt at something radically different, in that it aspires to interest those who know and care nothing for its author but who care about his theme. Like a poem or a novel, it struggles to exist for itself and in its own right.

Writing is a craft, even an art; and like other crafts and arts – carpentry or music, for example – it is learnt in stages. To write a thesis often marks the apprenticeship of a scholar: a period of transition where, though still a student, he is eagerly and hopefully demonstrating a claim to be something more. That is the sense in which it is almost necessarily an ambiguous exercise. Being a student, its author is accustomed to the attention of a teacher, and usually to a sympathetic attention. But he is also, and for the first time, writing for the world, or for some little part of it. And that is something he may be unaccustomed to doing or even trying to do. The revelation that the world can be indifferent to a work composed laboriously and out of sincere conviction may be a harsh one, and often is. It is always hard to realize that intensity of conviction, of itself, validates nothing. It can all too easily be seen as worthless: worthless not because it is false, since many false views are of vital importance in scholarly debate, but because it is trite. That realization may be called the hard landing of the apprentice scholar: to be told that his view, though earnestly and even passionately held, is of no interest to others. The student, as opposed to the scholar, is not used to being spoken to in that way. He is used to being encouraged. The scholar, by contrast, is entirely used to it. He is told it by implication every day of his life: when an editor or publisher returns a manuscript, when a letter of enquiry goes unanswered, or when a new and influential study by another scholar treats his own work as if it had never existed.

Like other kinds of authorship, scholarship is full of hard landings. It is not by nature a sympathetic world, or under any obligation to be so. It encourages, if at all, by criticism; it tests theses to destruction. None of that will deter the enthusiast for learning, who by definition will already know what it is to test-to-destruction the views of published scholars; and this book is written for just such enthusiasts, and by one.

Research can be fun. But it is fun only to those who know what it is and how it is run; and it makes no sense to enter a profession, or even to try to enter one, without noticing in advance the conditions that prevail there. Most people associate with authors the epithet 'struggling', and a struggle is what authorship necessarily is, especially at the start. No one will be interested in your views merely because they are yours. They will have to be presented lucidly, in correct formal dress, in a total awareness of the climate of opinion they exist in, and with a clear professional regard for the existing state of play. The apprentice may be forgiven mistakes, and mistakes are correctable. What he will not be forgiven is a manifest indifference to getting it right.

Many theses, unfortunately, do not look as if the author is even *trying* to get it right. They are internally incompatible in style – incompatible not just with any received system of presenting evidence, that is, but even with themselves. They openly proclaim an indifference. A thesis cannot afford to proclaim that. Being offered as a work of scholarship, it must at least look as if thought had been given to scholarly process and to an achieved consistency of presentation. No one will believe in it otherwise.

A thesis is not a self-expressive activity, since a scholar does not write to express himself. He writes to contribute to a scholarly dialogue already under way, and one where his contribution will inevitably be viewed as part of a larger whole, to be critically examined by minds that are themselves conscious of that larger whole. The beginner needs to take stock of that. The shift in schools and universities towards the extended essay or dissertation is meant to give him the chance to take stock. A self-expressive tone can be excused, even welcomed, in a script written in the conditions of a three-hour examination paper, where books are seldom allowed and where quotations are not expected to be referenced or even entirely accurate. None of those licences apply to the thesis. In formal terms, a thesis has to be right.

In its nature, then, a thesis is less free than other tasks; and to choose to write one is to take a step not into freedom but out of it. Its world is (rightly and inevitably) highly regulated and fully convention-bound. This book is about some of those rules and conventions, especially in its later chapters. The first step is to see that they are there, and that they need to be there. No one could so much as find his way about, in the world of scholarship, without them.

Such rules may be called the rational prejudices of scholarship; and 'without the aid of prejudice and custom,' as Hazlitt once remarked, 'I should not be able to find my way across the room.' Learning to be a scholar, for which writing a thesis is one of the commonest preparations, is rather like trying to find your way across the room. The child will bang its head or fall down, and it takes time to learn to avoid one such fate or the other. Even walking, that seemingly simple act, is something no one learnt all at once.

And scholarship is nothing like as simple as walking. In fact it is not simple at all.

CHAPTER TWO
Am I stupid enough?

He laughed heartily when I mentioned to him a saying of his
concerning Mr Thomas Sheridan, which Foote took a wicked pleasure
to circulate. 'Why, Sir, Sherry is dull, naturally dull; but it must have
taken him a great deal of pains to become what we now see him. Such
an excess of stupidity, Sir, is not in Nature.'

'So,' said he, 'I allowed him all his own merit.'

James Boswell, *Life of Samuel Johnson* (1791) for 28 July 1763

A man who has faith must be prepared not only to be a martyr, but
to be a fool.   G. K. Chesterton, *Heretics* (1905)

Radiguet discovered that it was better than countering habitual
assumptions to counter the *avant-garde*: with the innocent air of one
who is out of date, to move faster than the fastest that there are . . .
No more revolutionary attitude can be imagined, no greater audacity,
than this . . . He was delighted when we became distrusted by Right
and Left alike . . . Originality, he would say, consists in trying to
behave like everyone else without succeeding . . .

Such divine stupidity might well turn into the phenomenon known
as genius, where thought becomes deed and word is made flesh in a
single, startling operation that exemplifies Picasso's formula: 'The artist
first finds, and later seeks.'

Luther's *Gott ist dumm* would be the blasphemy to end all
blasphemies, were it not the praise to end all praise. By that famous
'God is stupid', Luther simply means that men cannot sensibly
attribute to Him their own miserable intelligence. God leaves the part
of the intellectual to the Devil.

Jean Cocteau, *Discours de réception à l'Académie Française* (1955)

The worst mistake, at the start, is to wonder or worry whether
you are intelligent enough.

In a sense, you can easily be too intelligent: too fast-thinking to
write things down as you think of them; too rapid in drawing

conclusions to verify them; too impatient to revise; and too lively in curiosity about the next question to be concerned enough with the last. As the mathematician G. H. Hardy once remarked of the creative life: 'For anything worth doing, intelligence is a very minor gift.' You can easily have too much of it – still more easily over-value others for having it at all. As a cure, the question to worry about is not 'Am I intelligent enough?' but 'Am I stupid enough?' It can be hard, especially for the educated, to slow the mind down and take stock of what one already knows.

If that question sounds unusual, it is because we live in thrall to an Intelligence Cult. School-leavers worry if they are intelligent enough to go to a university – imitating their parents and teachers, usually, who have already begun to worry about it loudly and in their hearing. Students in higher education worry about whether they are intelligent enough to impress not just their examiners and future employers, but even one another in ordinary conversation. And when it comes to writing a thesis, they worry about whether they are intelligent enough to choose a good topic – and then begin to worry about whether they are intelligent enough to do justice to it. They have been taught to worry about being intelligent: it would not occur to them to behave in any other way. And it will take some strenuous persuasion to convince them that they need not worry about it at all; still more to convince them that they should begin to worry about the reverse.

If intelligence means quick-wittedness, then an author can hardly afford to be intelligent. Writing is necessarily a slow and deliberate process. Even the quickest hand or fastest typewriter or word-processor cannot move at the speed of ordinary thought, or even of ordinary speech, let alone as fast as the speech or thought of the quick-thinking mind. To write is not to speed up, then, but to slow down; and an aspiring writer who worries about his own intelligence is only making his problem worse. It is rather like taking a costive for constipation.

Few minds are naturally paced for authorship. Boswell's *Life of Samuel Johnson* (1791), in its reported conversations, suggests that Johnson's gravely deliberate intelligence may have been an inter-esting exception. He had paced his mind down to something like dictation-speed: as people sometimes say, he talked like a book. But that is highly exceptional. Few of us think as well as we speak, or speak as well as we write; and the authorial art is a gently ruminative one, rather like a cow chewing cud – 'an effort of slow diligence,' as Johnson himself wrote in the *Adventurer* in March 1754, 'and steady perseverance' (no. 138). If you worry about being intelligent, you are unlikely ever to achieve such a pace of mind. The first need is not to speed up, then, but to slow down.

The second is to see that writing is not a single act but a process. It is not remotely spontaneous, and to speak of 'writing up' the results of research is to betray a total misunderstanding of how scholars work. Composing is not where they stop but where they start. It is only when words begin to appear on the page, whether as shorthand notes or as connected prose, that the mental activity of authorship begins at all. Writing is writing, not preparing to write. You cannot collect materials without knowing what they are for, or know what they are for without having written something. That is why writing begins *early* in any scholarly programme. It is not the end of a process, as beginners sometimes imagine to their cost, but the beginning of one.

Writing is largely rewriting. For all but a few, it is not in nature that any but the rarest sentence in a first draft should finally be allowed to stand. Authors may be divided into revisers and non-revisers; but where scholarly prose is concerned, it is so overwhelmingly probable that revision will be necessary that the non-reviser may realistically by dismissed, early in the argument, as likely to be little better than slipshod or incompetent. All scholarly prose improves with revision. That is why it helps here to be slow-paced of mind – a little stupid, in that special sense of the word, rather than bright, mercurial and quick. The scholar paces his mind downwards till it achieves what Johnson called slow diligence and steady perseverance. He knows he cannot hurry. He also knows that he need not hurry, since he will return some day to perfect what for the moment is the merest draft. He may even choose to leave spaces where words or phrases do not easily spring to mind: he will think of something later.

There are those who never learn slow diligence, and the Intelligence Cult may be blamed for the sad truth that they never learn it. Mistaking authorship for a single act, they imagine that they must be too stupid to write when they discover that, as a single act, they cannot do it. But the simple truth is that they are not yet stupid enough to write, and they make it worse by failing to see that they are not. 'I sometimes try to be miserable,' said the poet Blake, 'that I may do more work.' If being miserable means slowing down a little, then Blake's example is a good one, and (once realized) not hard to take. The more one thinks about it, in fact, the easier it is to take.

It is also, in its paradoxical way, cheerful advice. For if it is

creative to be miserable, then it is easy to be creative. If it is easy
not to be too intelligent, then it is easy for a writer to write. If
it is good to slow down, then one can forget a concern about
not being clever. Blake's advice is what every author needs. And his
adage helps one to see that one's worst moments can be one's best:
no need to push, no need to worry.

To write is to be dourly content with the modest powers one
already has. The Intelligence Cult has obscured that vital truth about
creativity. It depresses with a sense of inadequacy; it inhibits early
drafting, since those who wait for inspiration can wait for a long
time or forever. And because it inhibits drafting, which should begin
long before one has collected all, or even most, of the materials
needed, it frustrates the profound mental process of rethinking and
after-thinking that is among the richest rewards authorship has to
give.

Most good thoughts are afterthoughts. They come unawares,
often, when a first draft – perhaps nothing more than rapid notes
or unkempt prose – provokes a momentum of mind that needs no
further prompting to go on and on. It is in that mental mood
between first draft and second that real intelligence begins to sprout.
The German poet Kleist once spoke of the 'gradual fabrication' of
speech, by which we find ourselves saying more than we first knew
we had to say; and that gradual fabrication is even richer in writing
than in talking. Conversation gives you thoughts you did not know
you could think; writing enriches that gift, till you are positively
amazed you could think so much. That is why the Intelligence Cult,
in its most familiar form, is in the end so destructive to intelligence
itself; and why the advice to write before you know what to write,
odd as it sounds, is good advice.

The Intelligence Cult defeats intelligence itself. It mistakes sudden
inspiration for creativity; it glibly overvalues the flash of genius and
the dazzle of quick debate. But flash and dazzle are always likely to
be the end-products of quietude and slow deliberation: a good talker,
and especially a fast talker, is always likely to have thought much
of it out before, by ruminating it. And it is only in such rumination
that one is ever likely to see where the elements of an argument
properly belong, whether in talk or in scholarship – how they alter
other arguments, how they are to be ordered, and why they are
rightly there at all.

To be slow, then, can be a blessing. It can also be a distinction.
Those who write theses – or think about writing them – are often
highly intelligent beings at an advanced stage in the educational

10

process. No wonder they imagine they would be even better if they were more intelligent: it has probably never occurred to them to doubt it. But their quickness of mind is after all a commonplace attribute in the world they familiarly inhabit. That world – the world of thesis-writers – is full of intelligent people. The real task is much harder than to be intelligent. It is to unlearn all that, to relax and to slow down.

CHAPTER THREE
The fear of eccentricity

The Phoenicians set out from the Red Sea, and sailed south; and whenever autumn came, they would put in and sow the land, . . . and then await the harvest; then, having gathered in the crop, they sailed on. So that after two years had passed, they rounded the Pillars of Hercules in the third year and so returned to Egypt.

There they said what some may believe – though I do not – that in sailing [westward] round Africa, they had the sun on their right hand.

Herodotus IV.42

Leibniz . . . did work on mathematical logic which would have been enormously important, if he had published it; he would, in that case, have been the founder of mathematical logic, which would have become known a century and a half sooner than it did in fact.

He abstained from publishing, because he kept on finding evidence that Aristotle's doctrine of the syllogism was wrong on some points; respect for Aristotle made it impossible for him to believe this, so he mistakenly supposed that the errors must be his own.

Bertrand Russell, *History of Western Philosophy* (1946)

The Intelligence Cult has laid demands on its victims that are not merely misconceived but self-contradictory.

That is because, in its most familiar and competitive form, the cult arises as much out of a desire to be admired as out of an ambition to create. The Intelligence Cult is at heart a cult of socially acceptable intelligence.

But creative scholarship, like other kinds of creativity, need not be socially acceptable at all. It can be eccentric in its findings, in the estimation of its own age; disturbing, often enough, and sometimes simply repellent. There is no presumption that the truth about past or present is a reassuring or engaging truth. Some of the truths of

12

literary and political history are disquieting, and one might easily wish they had never been made; not least disquieting in questioning assumptions long held and firmly cherished.

No one should assume, then, that he will be admired or loved for having discovered something. At the least, he may be rejected as a crank; at the worst, reviled as an infidel. The results of research need not be socially acceptable at all, and people have been known to lose friends and make enemies by doing it, especially if they do it well. It is in that sense that the Intelligence Cult is self-contradictory. The free exercise of original intelligence need not be attractive at all, and it can be disturbing to show people what they do not want to know. Yet any intellectual enquiry, if it is genuinely that, cannot in conscience stop at the point where it threatens to lose itself friends. If it means what it claims to mean, then it must go on. That is the point where the researcher needs to be courageous as well as intelligent – to realize (if he has not already realized it) that research takes courage.

Courage enters the question even at its first stage, in the choice of a subject. There is little point in writing a thesis about what everybody already knows and already believes. Research is supposed to *make a difference*, after all, to what everybody already knows or believes, even if only a tiny difference. It is pointless to plant a flag with an air of discovery at the end of Brighton pier. Making a difference, in that sense, can only mean pointing to a deficiency, a weakness or a fault.

It is with that sense of a deficiency, or worse, that the impulse to research most naturally begins. As an impulse, it can easily be strangled at birth by a fear of eccentricity, presumption or even arrogance. The young researcher, especially, may amiably wonder to himself who in the world he thinks himself to be, to question learned opinion or the common assumptions of his age. But if he heeds that amiable scruple, then he is not a researcher, and he had better take his amiability elsewhere. Research demands presumption. There would be no point in writing at all if the question were already fully answered or widely understood. And if it is arrogant to think the world in its collective wisdom to be occasionally mistaken, then you will need to be arrogant too.

Sainte-Beuve once remarked that the origin of all discovery was to be 'amazed by what seems simple to the majority of mankind'. The thesis-writer needs to be at least occasionally amazed by what seems simple – even obvious – to all or most learned opinion. That is where the itch to research best begins. It may seem obvious to learned opinion that there was an artistic Renaissance in fifteenth- and sixteenth-century Europe, or that nineteenth-century England had a working class, and even a 'working-class literature', or that socialism and racialism have always been opposed, or that Virginia Woolf was a great novelist. But if all that seems simple or obvious to learned opinion, then it may be for the researcher to follow Sainte-Beuve's precept, if he is worth his salt at all, and allow himself to be amazed. Such propositions, it is possible, only seem obvious because they are often repeated and often taken for granted. One can hardly expect to make friends by doubting any of them; and the risk of being thought eccentric, or something worse, is all too clear. That is why courage is needed in research even in its opening stages, when a topic is chosen.

The task of destroying shibboleths is rightly seen as a task for the brave, but it has no business to allow itself to be seen as cynical. There is nothing cynical about setting out to destroy the illusions of an age, even if the destruction of cherished beliefs causes embarrassment and even pain. Destructive criticism can be highly idealistic in its motives. When Humphry House wrote *The Dickens World* (1941), a book that proved to be the foundation of Dickens studies for a whole generation, he was moved by a hatred of Dickens's social views, and even a contempt for his art, that derived from a highly idealistic vision of how a society should be ordered if it is ever to be called just. No one need share that vision to applaud either the motive or the outcome. *The Dickens World* is a noble work, whatever one may think of the cogency of its assumptions or conclusions. It is also a destructive work: dismissive of the affectionate triviality, as House saw it, of existing Dickens criticism, and of the unquestioning hero-worship that had largely vitiated Dickens studies since his death in 1870.

Since House was a man of virtue as well as erudition, the case may be seen as a paradigm. It has never been in doubt that his *Dickens World* was destructive in intent and in effect, though not only that; and it is not in doubt, equally, that its author's motives were high-minded. In scholarship, then, the creative instinct and the destructive need not be far apart. On occasion they can be one. It may be useful to take stock of that uncomfortable truth at an early stage.

Not all historical questions are as bitterly contested as Dickens's social views, but few that are worth considering are without contest. It would be unusual to find a thesis-topic that lacked its destructive aspect. Great art, as F. Scott Fitzgerald once remarked in his notes, is 'the contempt of a great man for small art'; and great scholarship is similarly the contempt of a great scholar for the lesser sort. You write because you think you can do better. If the issue or the author are familiar and much discussed, then it is not over-sceptical to suppose that some of the discussion has been less than wise; if little discussed, as in the case of some minor problem, author, or historical event, then the very lack of discussion may indicate an inadequacy that the thesis is eager to expose and correct. Research is performed to right a wrong, whether of commission or omission, to justify a reasonable grudge, or to correct a failing. If it is not, then it is hard to see what reason it has to be attempted at all. It is certainly not a blandly appreciative act that purposes to leave matters much as before. The most inadequate of all grounds for researching an author is that one likes him. It may be one thing to like him, in any case, and another to like what he has written. 'Sometimes I read a book with pleasure', said Jonathan Swift, 'and detest the author.' Liking may be no bad ground for studying; but research is not the same as study.

The insistence may sometimes be seen as disagreeable, though it is nothing of the kind. House's *Dickens World* is not a disagreeable book, or a book written out of unworthy motives. There is a world of difference between condemning a view and condemning the author of that view, though some scholars to the end of their days never manage to learn it. One might very well reject Shakespeare's view of autocracy, or Milton's of divine redemption, without rejecting Shakespeare or Milton: one might certainly reject those views, what is more, without seeking to diminish the standing of either of them as great poets. What natural presumption is there that great writers say nothing but true things? William Empson believed that *Paradise Lost* was all the greater a poem because its view of divine providence was barbarous, and the greater still because (as he believed) Milton himself could partly see that it was so; and he wrote *Milton's God* (1961) to prove it. To attack an author on grounds as momentous as these is not to diminish him. It is to enhance an interest and enrich a debate.

The highest tribute we can pay to a doctrine, in the end, is to concede that it has risen to the dignity where it deserves to be called into question – to be tested, exposed, and even (in extreme cases) refuted. All of which suggests that the fear of eccentricity that dogs many a timid young researcher is one he is well advised to forget. Scholarship is a world for the polite, since one can be polite even in refutation. But it is not a world for the demure.

CHAPTER FOUR
The lure of theory

It is not certain that everything is uncertain.

Pascal, *Pensées* (1670 etc.)

If the creator of the universe had chosen to make a world full of compartments divided by walls touching the heavens, had put into each of those cells a savage race – if at some future time the progress of science had enabled men to scale those walls – I won't say but that this would have been an interesting world.

We imagine the enquirer passing from cell to cell, examining the present state of its inmates, exploring their past history as recorded by documents which range from the chipped flint to the printed book. After a while he begins to know what he will find in the next box – 'Ah! I thought so: promiscuity, group-marriage, exogamy – fetishism, polytheism, monotheism, positivism – picture writing, ideogram, phonogram, ink, block-books, movable type – the old tale.' After a while he has got a law – 'What, no evidence of a polytheistic stage in this country! I supply that stage with certainty; the evidence must have been lost.' He comes to a more puzzling case where, twist the evidence how he will, it breaks his law. But by this time he is justified in using such terms as 'morbid', 'abnormal', 'retrogression' – here is a diseased community and he will investigate the climate of the cell, and so forth, in order to get at the cause of the disease. There remain many compartments with walls so high that they are still insurmountable. 'Considering my many thousands of observations,' he says, 'I feel entitled to make a scientific prediction as to what is behind these barriers – in some cases I shall be wrong, and to details I will not commit myself – but in general I shall be right.'

A very interesting world this would be, but exceedingly unlike the world in which we live. In the real world, the political organisms have been and are so few, and the history of each of them has been so unique, that we have no materials apt for an induction of this sort, we have no means of forming the idea of the *normal* life of a body politic.

. . . We do not know, if I may so put it, that Siamese twins are abnormal . . . .

I have a special dread of those theorists who are trying to fill up the dark ages of medieval history with laws collected from the barbarian tribes that have been observed in modern days. This procedure urges me to ask: if the tribes of which you speak are on the normal high-road of progress, why have they not by this time gone further along it? If I see a set of trucks standing on a railway line from week to week, I do not say 'This is the main line up to London'. I say 'This must be a siding'. The traveller who has studied the uncorrupted savage can often tell the historian of medieval Europe what to look for, never what to find.

F. W. Maitland, '*The body politic*' (written c.1899)

We confuse the world 'indefinable' with the word 'vague'. If some one speaks of a spiritual fact as 'indefinable', we promptly picture something misty – a cloud with indeterminate edges. But this is an error even in commonplace logic.

The thing that cannot be defined is the first thing: the primary fact. It is our arms and legs, our pots and pans, that are indefinable. The indefinable is the indisputable. The man next door is indefinable, because he is too actual to be defined.

G. K. Chesterton, *Charles Dickens* (1906)

Three beliefs pervade most modern accounts of scientific principles and are the principal source of confusion. The first is that in some sense scientific laws are statements made with certainty. The second is that physical measures can be exact. The third is that there is a clearly marked boundary between science and ordinary thought . . .

The first of these fallacies was sufficiently refuted by Hume . . . The second fallacy ignores observational errors . . .

An instance of the third is the rejection of colour under the description 'secondary quality' . . . If we do, an analytical chemist or a field botanist can no longer use his colour sensations . . . But he knows quite well that colour sensation is good enough for his purpose.

Harold Jeffreys, *Scientific Inference* (3rd edition, 1973)

The past, or for that matter the present, may be studied in detail or as a single whole. And glimpses of a single whole are called theory.

Theories of history or the arts have a double appeal, and in a paradoxical sense. One is that they appear to offer a release from the thrall of detail; the other, that they offer a scheme or framework to which details may be attached. In either event, the theorist can be a happy man. Where theory is a short-cut, it can dismiss the study of mere detail as irrelevant pedantry, since the truth is already known

17

– at least in outline. Or detail can be embraced and cherished, piled high to confirm a truth already known and already proclaimed.

In literary studies, as in social and political history, a passion for theory is sometimes seen as a mark of the modern mind, though it is hard to see why. Even on the evidence of surviving texts, theoretical criticism began in Europe with Plato and Aristotle, which makes it older than literary history by some two thousand years. If it counts as a theory to study history and biography as a system of contrasting vices and virtues, as in Plutarch's lives, then historical theory is at least as old as the history of events. And the Whig interpretation of history, which flourished for some two centuries after the English Revolution of 1689, was plainly a *theory* of political history, whether acceptable or not.

That is not altogether what we have lately been encouraged to believe. But then modern theories of history like those of the Annales school in France, or theories of literature such as Deconstruction, often flourish through a cultivated reputation for intellectual chic, conveniently dubbing their opponents as traditionalists. The study of literary history is not at all ancient in the European tradition, compared with critical theory: it is scarcely older in its continuous tradition than the eighteenth century. Odd that it should be thought of as old-fashioned, then. Odd too, that sociology or linguistics should be seen as new: they were highly active interests of the European Enlightenment; and even in the eighteenth century they were not exactly new in themselves, though they were adopting ever-changing forms.

Whether large or small, a theoretical topic may be as good as any other for a thesis. Ancient as it is, being at least as old as Plato, literary theory is an entirely respectable study. Some of the conditions under which it may survive and continue to flourish are set out here, for clarity's sake, in numbered order.

1. The study of theory needs to be as rigorously handled as any other kind of study. It is not a leap into a void; it liberates no one from the demand for sufficient evidence or a convincing sequence of argument. It needs to be as good as anything else: as firmly based on data as anything else, such as historical evidence and a sufficiency of instances. A theory of tragedy, for example, would need to embrace all the instances of tragedy that there are, and one counter-instance would be fatal to it. Those who embrace theoretical questions under the illusion that they offer a blank cheque to personal speculation, or allow or encour-

age a neglect of detail or counter-argument, are justly disappointed by what they find there. As an area of study, theory is at least as constraining as fact.

2. Since theory is ancient, in historical and literary studies, it needs to be seen as that, if the grave charge of provincialism is to be avoided. Nothing is new because it is called that; and theories called new, like the French *Nouvelle Critique* of the 1960s, can be rather like a stockmarket tip or a racing tip: by the time they reach you they are unlikely to be the latest thing, and are far more likely to have been discounted by expert opinion. By the time you have written and submitted your thesis, they will be older still. Today's trend – inevitably – is tomorrow's old hat.

There is a provincialism of time as well as of place, and it consists of assuming that an idea that looks new, or is called new, is likely to be that. The American New Criticism of the 1940s, the New Left of the 1960s, and the *Nouvelle Critique* that supplanted both, bore titles that should have invited scepticism from the start, much as they would on advertising boards. The French New Critics were often provincials in that style: they imagined that theories of language they had only recently encountered, like the linguistic theory that words are arbitrary signs, must be new in substance. They confused 'new' with 'new to them'. (In fact the Arbitrariness of the Sign was a doctrine familiar to Aristotle, Aquinas and Shakespeare). Like brand-names in commercial advertising, critical theories are often marketed as new when their substance is old: it is an approved way of moving out old stock. That is how goods are sold to the innocent; and the self-promoting techniques of recent theorists might in themselves provide a good topic for research, to the strong-minded.

3. A theory is a theory of something, and that something needs to be called in evidence if the theory is to survive at all. A theory of fiction, in literary terms, is a theory about what novelists and others have in fact done; and if a novel can be found that does not conform to it, then it is the theory – not the novel – that is at fault. The definitions of literary kinds supplied by Northrop Frye in his *Anatomy of Criticism* (1957) are as good as the instances make them; and no instance has to move over, or be reclassified, to conform to them. Theories of history like the Whig or the Marxist are about what happened, not about what ought to have happened if humanity were tidier in its affairs; and counter-instances such as societies unmoved by class war need to be heard for the prosecution. And a theory of tragedy that excluded *King*

Lear or included *Charley's Aunt* would be a dud theory, no matter how imposing or ingenious in itself. Art is under no obligation to attend to what theorists say; neither are political and social events.

4. A theory cannot afford to contradict itself. If all views are governed by social conditioning, then the views of political scientists too are so governed; and if it can be shown to be otherwise, then the exception is fatal to the theory. If language cannot describe reality, as Deconstructionists have claimed, then the language of Deconstructionists, too, is non-descriptive: in which case they have failed to describe the reality of language. If men love freedom, why – or under what conditions – do they choose slavery or adulate dictators? Easy theories flourish through a lack of rigour; and the task of the modern theorist is to expose facile arguments and to test assumptions that are glibly and fashionably made.

5. One fundamental example of self-contradiction may be conveniently called positivism, or the view that questions of fact are objective and questions of value are not. But if values are merely personal or subjective, then positivism too is merely that, since it claims to be better than other arguments; and to claim to be better is itself a value-judgment. Unless, of course, positivists can offer some convincing ground why their claim to possess a better argument than another can be shown to be exempt from itself.

6. The view that value-judgments are merely subjective, whether in art or morality, is often confidently sustained on several familiar supports, and all of them are unsound.

   One is that we have no agreement on such matters. But this claim, even if it were to the point, is false. In the Western world, for example, we have agreement that slavery is wrong, which is a moral judgment; just as in earlier ages there was agreement that it was not. Either way, these are instances of moral agreement. In the arts, similarly, we have agreement that Shakespeare was a great dramatist and Beethoven a great composer. Those who claim that value-judgments in morality or in the arts never achieve unanimity of sentiment, then, can be shown on plain evidence to be mistaken.

7. The second familiar support is that an objective question is one on which all men agree, or can be induced to agree. But that, too, is mistaken. Scientists do not agree about the physical sciences

– about how the cosmos began, for example – and yet it is not usually thought to follow that the nature and history of the physical universe are subjective questions. Population experts disagree about the population of China in any given year, but that population is what it is. We do not need agreement about a question to suppose it to be an objective one.

8. The third familiar support is the claim that what we cannot answer, we do not know. Since we cannot explain why Shakespeare is a great dramatist, or Beethoven a great composer, and in sufficient terms, then (it is sometimes suggested) we do not certainly know that they are.

But there is a good deal that we know, and even certainly know – and outside the worlds of morality or the arts – which we cannot put into words. We know the taste of familiar foods, for example, to the extent that we can answer accurately what they are, though blindfold; and yet we remain unable to explain how we distinguish one from the other, even though we distinguish them infallibly. We may know how to ride a bike without being able to explain, in sufficient terms, why we do not fall off; though in that case it is true that an expert could explain in technical terms why we do not fall off, and independently of whether he can ride one himself or not. To know such matters may, on occasion, be accompanied by an ability to explain, but it plainly does not *depend* on a ability to explain. It is no objection, then, to the claims of Shakespeare or Beethoven to say we cannot justify them in words, and in sufficient terms; it is bad theory to suppose that we only know what we can express, or that what we cannot express we do not know.

These are all theoretical questions and theoretical debates, and it is not in doubt that the study of past and present has a lively place for theory. It has long had such a place. Plutarch, Sir Joshua Reynolds, and the great Whig historians like Macaulay were theorists – among other things. They made theoretical assertions, that is, and theoretical assumptions. This is an ancient activity of the Western mind: a good deal more ancient, it may well be, than the history of events, or the detailed study of literary history, or the lives of artists and composers. Plato's view in the *Republic* that poets – or rather the authors of fiction – should be expelled from his ideal state is a theory of art, and it is answered in Aristotle's *Poetics*. The question which of them was right, or to what extent one or the other was right, remains an active question; much as the total number of elements in the physical universe – another problem proposed by the Ancients – remains active. Theory has its place in modern research, and a thesis may well be theoretical.

But a good thesis would bring as much scepticism to bear upon theories, ancient or modern, as upon the study of particular events or particular authors. And it would not commit the elementary and provincial error of supposing that critical theory, whether in history or the arts, was an invention of our own times.

CHAPTER FIVE
Choosing a theme

'What a useful thing a pocket-map is!' I remarked.

'That's another thing we've learned from your nation,' said Mein Herr, 'map-making. But we've carried it much further than you. What do you consider the largest map that would be really useful?'

'About six inches to the mile.'

'Only six inches!' exclaimed Mein Herr. 'We very soon got to six yards to the mile. Then we tried a hundred yards to the mile. And then came the grandest idea of all! We actually made a map of the country on the scale of a mile to the mile!'

'Have you used it much?' I enquired.

'It has never been spread out, yet,' said Mein Herr: 'the farmers objected.'

Lewis Carroll, *Sylvie and Bruno Concluded* (1893)

The belief that we can start with pure observations alone, without anything in the nature of a theory, is absurd; as may be illustrated by the story of the man who dedicated his life to natural science, wrote down everything he could observe, and bequeathed his priceless collection of observations to the Royal Society to be used as inductive evidence. This story should show us that though beetles may profitably be collected, observations may not.

Twenty-five years ago I tried to bring home the same point to a group of physics students in Vienna by beginning a lecture with the following instructions: 'Take pencil and paper; carefully observe, and write down what you have observed!' They asked, of course, *what* I wanted them to observe. Clearly the instruction 'Observe!' is absurd. . . . Observation is always selective. It needs a chosen object, a definite task, an interest, a point of view, a problem.

Karl Popper, 'Science: conjectures and refutations' (1953) in his
Conjectures and Refutations (1963)

The secret springs of the pleasure which good versification can give is little explored by critics: a few pages of Coventry Patmore and a few of Frederic Myers contain all, so far as I know, or all of value, which has been written on such matters.

[Footnote] I mean such matters as these: the existence in some metres, not in others, of an inherent alternation of stresses, stronger and weaker; the presence in verse of silent and invisible feet, like rests in music; the reason why some lines of different length will combine harmoniously, while others can only be so combined by great skill or good luck; why, while blank verse can be written in lines of ten or six syllables, a series of octosyllables ceases to be verse if they are not rhymed; how Coleridge, in applying the new principle which he announced in the preface to 'Christabel', has fallen between two stools; the necessary limit to inversion of stress, which Milton understood and Bridges overstepped; why, of two pairs of rhymes, equally correct and both consisting of the same vowels and consonants, one is richer to the mental ear and the other poorer; the office of alliteration in verse, and how its definition must be narrowed if it is to be something which can perform that office and not fail of its effect or actually defeat its purpose.

A. E. Housman, *The Name and Nature of Poetry* (1933)

Research is performed in order to be used, and used by somebody else.

It is not a self-regarding activity, or an exercise in sincerity. Even if in the event it is not used, it is still meant to be: meant to tell some one something he did not know or understand, and something he needed or wanted to know or understand. A research subject, in fact, is a response to the climate of opinion one lives in; and it necessarily, for that reason, depends on some acquired sense of other minds – their puzzles, preoccupations and fears.

The way to choose a theme, then, is to listen to others, and (if passive listening is not enough) to ask. A subject is a good one if it supplies a demand or a deficiency that other minds have already revealed. That includes the minds of those who teach. Those who teach do not just know more answers than those who learn: they know more questions too. In fact a beginner can hardly be expected to know what the unanswered questions are, and he needs to attend carefully if he is ever to learn what they are.

Listening to others does not imply doing what you are told; and to ask openly for a thesis-topic is rightly understood to betray a lack of wit. But then paying attention to what others say is not – or not necessarily – believing what they say. Disbelief in others can be a spur: 'Why in the world do you think that?' And disbelief demands at least as much attention as belief – perhaps more. If you do not attend, you will not disagree. If the topic emerges as the refutation of a myth, then the myth will need to be carefully heeded and pondered if it is ever to be given full weight and justice.

In research in the humanities, the beginner sometimes needs to be strenuously persuaded that there are significant questions still demanding to be answered. That is because he has usually been schooled in a tradition that implies answers are always to be had, if only one knows where to look for them. Class-room teaching is normally concerned with what is already known, seldom with what is so far unknown. Tempting to imagine, then, that the study of history or the arts is more or less fully realized, the still unanswered questions being more or less trivial. It is easy to be over-impressed by the imposing weight of scholarship that already exists – and, for that matter, by the triviality of topics that researchers sometimes suppose themselves forced, in self-protection, to adopt. The student can waste years in convincing himself of something that every working scholar knows already: that many of the greatest subjects of research are in fact ill provided for, or not provided for at all; that many unanswered questions have been simply ignored; that many unedited texts need editions; that many theoretical issues have been all too rashly 'solved'; and that many highly elementary questions remain to this day utterly unattempted.

The issue is to see what they are. It will be unavoidable here, in the first instance, to gesture towards large problems and wide areas of study – problems and areas plainly too large and too wide for a single thesis. But properly considered, scale is not in the end a difficulty, or at least not an insuperable one. A thesis-topic, being part of a greater endeavour, is commonly best seen as a fragment of something more than itself; and the objection that the unexplored fields of research are too big for the beginner to tackle is not, after due consideration, an objection at all. The larger needs are properly considered first, and well before a choice is made. The next step is to distinguish some specific aspect of the problem, where an individual contribution might be made. No wonder if, at the start, great research areas look rugged and mountainous; but it may still be possible to find a square yard to work in. The first job is to find the mountain.

Renaissance English – the English of Shakespeare, Jonson, Bacon and Hooker – still lacks a grammar and a dictionary, at least as grammars and dictionaries are understood in the late twentieth century; though some of these authors have attracted individual gloss-aries and concordances to allow one to find one's way about in them. Classical Greek and Latin have long enjoyed such aids; so have Old English and Middle English, and of course modern English. But Renaissance English, which some would call the greatest of all literary languages, has dropped through the crack, by a sort of scholarly inadvertence, and still waits to be described. A crucial word, then, or group of words, especially if it highlights a major intellectual debate of the sixteenth and seventeenth century, could well be a subject.

There are studies of metre for the great literary languages such as English, but few of them stretch far into the twentieth century. In 1933, in *The Name and Nature of Poetry*, A. E. Housman proposed a number of metrical questions that are still unanswered (see p. 23, above). Anyone who wants to discover what T. S. Eliot metrically performed, or Yeats, Auden or Dylan Thomas, would have to take a pencil and do it for himself. A serious metrical study of a single major poem by such a poet would at least offer a start. Literary translation, too, is a neglected area of research, and unexplainably so – and even more in the field of literary prose than in that of verse: possibly because it requires a good knowledge of more than one language. To realize how neglected, it is only necessary to recall that the philosopher Hobbes translated Thucydides (1629) and Homer (1673), an aspect of his literary achievement almost never mentioned.

There are multitudinous studies of the moral convictions and assumptions of great novelists, and of the imaginative patterns that emerge, consciously or unconsciously, from their novels. Such studies stretch out in long lines on library shelves, *ad tedium*. But there are far fewer that attempt to describe what they do with words, how their dialogue represents speech-usages like intonation, how objects are depicted in their fiction and take on symbolic value, or how (syntactically speaking) novels begin and end. Henry James magisterially posed many of the great issues of fictional form in his New York prefaces of 1907–9, collected after his death as *The Art of the Novel* (1934); but he was opening such issues, not closing them. The starting paragraph of a great novel might richly repay study in formal stylistic terms.

The history and literature of recent years is notably under-studied in any scholarly manner, simply because it is recent. There is no extensive synoptic history of early twentieth-century literature, for example; and J. I. M. Stewart's *Eight Modern Writers* (1963), the final volume of the Oxford History of English Literature, was based on the principle that it was still too early to tell so immediate a story, opting rather for essays on individual authors. In our own times, since 1945, the matter is still more open. In the nature of things there are seldom critical accounts of recent books or events, outside newspapers and periodicals. An historical crisis of the last dozen years, a new play, or a recent parliamentary debate – such matters are almost certainly untouched in academic terms, as opposed to journalistic terms. It would be a bold stroke to choose a recent event in history, and especially one armed with all the drama of conflict, and to describe it not in the language of a newspaper but with the scholarly hindsight of an historian.

Public prose, as opposed to specifically literary prose like essays, plays and novels, is massively neglected by literary historians, and not always much discussed by political historians either. There are many studies of Winston Churchill, but none of Churchill as a prose writer – even though he wrote a novel, was perhaps the greatest orator of his age, and won a Nobel Prize for Literature. There are many studies of Maynard Keynes, but no literary study – though he was arguably as good a prose writer as any in England in the years between two world wars, and easily better than many an overrated novelist of the age. Is there any study in the tradition of literary criticism of any House of Commons debate, old or new? Oratory is an art, and one closely linked to the events of its day, so that research into oratory might be thought attractive either to an historian or to a literary critic, though in practice it seems to attract neither; and doubly attractive to one who is both. Maurice F. Bond's *Guide to the Records of Parliament* (1972) is a thread through the labyrinth of Westminster records, and Hansard is a report of debates in both chambers, Lords and Commons, singularly unused by historians of literature. Why not a thesis, then, on some notable exchange there, such as the lively debate on capital punishment in the Commons in August 1983? It was settled on a free vote, and its reported speeches might reveal significant differences of vocabulary and syntax between speakers of different parties and divergent convictions concerning death by the rope.

Periodicals are a largely untapped source. A distinct segment of a great and famous periodical, like the first five years of *Punch* (1841–46) under its radical editor Douglas Jerrold, would make a theme for research; so would the entire run of many a little review. These have been difficult to find until recent years, unless one has a local supply; but a flood of directories in our times, some of them described in Chapter 8 below, makes the matter suddenly easy by listing periodicals with their locations, and even secondary materials describing them.

Drama is much studied in schools of literature; theatre less so, and especially recent theatre – at least in the formal style expected of a thesis. But plays are a fascinating textual study all of their own. Their texts can evolve from early drafts through rehearsals, where actors and producers as well as playwrights join in moulding the text, and that text does not always remain stable even after it is first printed. In a recent study of Tom Stoppard's *Night and Day* (1978), for example, Philip Gaskell, in an article in *Textual Criticism and Literary Interpretation* edited by Jerome J. McGann (1985), has illustrated the gradual evolution of a recent theatrical text in a study partly based on taped interviews with playwright, producer and actors.

Bibliography is a word with an iron ring, but anyone who has profited from the unique literary information to be found in such books as Richard L. Purdy's *Thomas Hardy: a bibliographical study* (1954) or David Gilson's *A Bibliography of Jane Austen* (1982) will learn to distrust its unhappy reputation for remote technicality. It can be the quickest path there is to literary enlightenment.

And to publication. Publishers' series like the Soho Bibliographies need more titles than they have, and anyone who could show a competence in small matters, like a single phase in the career of a twentieth-century poet or novelist, might find himself engaged in an apprenticeship to something larger. Publishers, collectors, booksellers and librarians are avid for information about how early editions differ, especially in the rich and untapped field of twentieth-century studies. A single work, like the extensive revisions to Evelyn Waugh's *Brideshead Revisited* (1945, revised in 1960 with a new preface) would be a hopeful point of entry.

There is little academic research into radio and television drama, and what there is can be vitiated by intellectual snobbery: a disdain for popular series merely because they are popular, and an excessive emphasis on Dylan Thomas's *Under Milk Wood* (1954) or the radio plays of Louis MacNeice. The connections between radio sitcom and the traditions of theatrical comedy are essentially unexplored; beyond Barry Took's *Laughter in the Air* ((1976, revised 1981) there is not much that has been independently written on broadcast comedy at all; and not much on TV drama, beyond Shaun Sutton's *The Largest Theatre in the World* (1982), a study of thirty years of BBC television by an experienced director.

Beginners sometimes imagine they should choose an author or a theme they enjoy. That is a natural assumption for them to make, and a mistaken one: a thesis is an exercise in analysis, not in affection, and demonstrations that great works are indeed that commonly emerge looking trite. Choosing a thesis-topic is not like choosing a husband or wife, and a topic need not be attractive at all. Affection, in this context, is a bad guide, if only because nobody wants to be told at length how admirable something is, especially if he knows it already.

But there is another, and more personal, reason why affection can mislead. Enthusiasms can easily cool as work advances. An analytical exercise, by contrast, can grow in interest as it goes. Revealing the unrevealed is an exciting task, and it can mount in excitement as it proceeds, by its own momentum. And it is far, far better to live with a mounting enthusiasm than with a fading one. The sheer stamina required by research will demand nothing less. Nothing intrinsically the matter, then, and nothing cynical, in choosing a topic out of a motive other than love.

To research is to answer a question, or at least to seek an answer. It is not to study it. Study is an indispensable preliminary to research, and no more than that. It is in that sense, above all, that writing a thesis is a radically distinct act from anything one is is likely to have done before. It is not like writing a better essay than usual. A thesis is not a kind of essay at all. A student essay may reasonably summarize what is known about the matter, and then stop. If that is what it does, then a thesis begins at the point where an essay ends. It is not essentially about what is already known: it is about what is unknown, or unrealized, or misinterpreted. It is concise in its account of familiar materials, for just that reason, and expansive only when the crucial point at issue is reached.

And it is that crucial point at issue – the problem or question that the thesis poses, enlarges on, and tries to solve or answer – that constitutes the heart of what it does, and the only reason it has, in the end, to exist at all.

CHAPTER SIX
Arranging it

Look what thy memory cannot contain
Commit to these waste blanks, and thou shalt find
Those children nursed, delivered from thy brain,
To take a new acquaintance of thy mind.
    These offices, so oft as thou wilt look,
    Shall profit thee, and much enrich thy book.
                    William Shakespeare, Sonnet 77

He told me that Bishop Mainwaring of St David's preached his
doctrine; for which, among others, he was sent prisoner to the Tower.
    Then thought Mr Hobbes, ''Tis time now for me to shift for
myself,' and so withdrew into France, and resided at Paris. As I
remember, there were others likewise did preach his doctrine. This
little manuscript treatise grew to be his book *De Cive*, and at last grew
there to be the so formidable *Leviathan*; the manner of writing of
which book, he told me, was thus. He walked much and
contemplated, and he had in the head of his staff a pen and ink-horn,
carried always a notebook in his pocket; and as soon as a thought
darted, he presently entered it into his book, or otherwise he might
perhaps have lost it. He had drawn the design of the book into
chapters etc, so he knew whereabout it would come in. Thus that
book was made.
                    John Aubrey, *Brief Lives*

It perpetually happens that one writer tells less truth than another,
merely because he tells more truths.
                    Thomas Babington Macaulay, '*History*' (1828)

There are three stages to scholarly authorship.
    The first is finding something to say; the second is arranging it;
the third expressing it. The division is an ancient one. Classical and

Renaissance rhetoricians called them *inventio, dispositio* and *elocutio* – finding, arranging, and expressing – and the division draws attention to a truth easily forgotten and even unnoticed: that writing is not just having something to say and saying it. There is a middle phase; and that middle phase, or *dispositio*, is in modern times by far the most neglected of the three. Some who approach thesis-writing for the first time do not even know that it is there.

It is easy for some one who has never attempted anything longer than an essay to suppose that a thesis will only demand of him that he should have something interesting to say, and that he should then say it. If he does, he may discover that problems of arrangement come upon him unawares and find him incapable of solving them. But a thesis needs to be in the right order as well as right; and the ordering of the chapters, and of sections within chapters, can be fundamental to its success. Even if, like T. S. Eliot's *Sacred Wood* (1920) or Lewis Namier's *Avenues of History* (1952), the final order were to amount to little more than a collection of independent essays, those essays would still need to be marshalled in an intelligible order and to be clearly organized within themselves. The work as a whole is unintelligible if they are not.

The first need, and the most urgent, is to see where the subject begins and ends. A thesis is not a statement of all your intellectual interests, or even of most of them. It answers a question plainly implied by your title and bluntly posed in your first chapter, and then it stops. It should not begin with Plato and end with Wittgenstein, and on the sole pretext that you have something interesting to say about Plato and Wittgenstein. Beginning with a specific question, it ends with an answer to it. It is not even meant to represent the range of your mental interests: like a blood sample, it leaves the greater part behind. Nor need it include a statement of one's profoundest beliefs about life, literature or history. Though it may suggest and imply all sorts of beliefs, it is not in itself a credo, and one's deepest convictions about this world or the next need find no place in it.

For just these reasons, there are no marks for length; though many, and rightly so, for brevity. Since a thesis answers the question posed, and not all the questions that there are, it can only profit from economy, and the prescribed word-limit is a blessing to the student as well as to the examiner. One does not usually say more by using more words; and a reading of critics and historians must long since have made it clear to you, as a reader, that it is so. Nor is it credible to suppose that one can only say what is to be said by bursting a word-limit, or even by reaching eagerly towards it. Such limits are limits, in any case, not targets; and because they are that, there can be no reasonable ground for straining to achieve them. A natural scientist recently won a Nobel Prize for an 800-word article in the periodical *Nature*.

If a Nobel Prize can be won on fewer than a thousand words, then a literary or historical point can be made in little more. It is a matter of achieving due critical severity with the use of evidence and supporting arguments. Private notes may be supported with the rich evidence of reading, and it may be all too easy to be reluctant to waste any of it. But dumping notes into finished prose is a precept for never finishing, or for finishing badly. Selection starts at once, even as one reads; and notes at their fullest represent nothing more, in the end, than a work-process. Nor are they wasted because in the end they are unused. Their use was to bring your mind to the point where they do not need to be used – where you can see that they are inessential, and why they are. And it is only because you once thought them to be essential that you can now see them to be otherwise.

There is every merit, in fact, in writing short. Most first drafts are too long, and they can easily represent time wasted where it could have been well used. If your temperament is happily the reverse of that, and your early drafts are too succinct, then it can be the easiest thing in the world to dilute them later, page by page, with supporting arguments and evidence, given that the essential structure of argument is already there. No need to be concerned, then, with a meagre first draft. As with instant coffee, it is the easiest thing in the world to pour on boiling water.

Writing short can be the best of all faults. And if the final version remains short, there may be no great harm in that. What counts is what it says, and whether it clearly says it. Most readers and examiners will be grateful for its brevity, and they may give to each page a more searching and respectful attention when they realize that its author is not one to waste words. Some readers, indeed, will demand nothing less than a disciplined brevity of utterance if they are to read at all. 'If it's on two pages,' a Prime Minister once remarked, 'I'll read it. If on five, my secretary will read it. If on more than five, no one will read it.' A scholarly reader is likely to be less stringent than a prime minister in his demand for brevity, but he sometimes envies him; and scholarly authors in our time need to know and remember that they always write for a busy and impatient world.

How should material be arranged?

The first step is to realize that you, and no one else, will need to arrange it. It will not arrange itself. A method may be borrowed or invented; but one way or another, it will have to be there. Notes do not order themselves, and there are few things more dispiriting than a fat pile of unarranged notes, especially if they are on sheets of different size. This is a problem to take stock of before beginning at all.

Stocktaking begins with a draft table of contents. It is a table that commits you to nothing: you may alter, add and subtract, and it would be surprising if you did not do all those things before you are finished. The table of contents is that page of the thesis that will, in all probability, register before you end the most numerous changes of mind. But you cannot change your mind until you have a mind to change, and you cannot see what is the matter with an arrangement until it has been tried on a single sheet – still less estimate how to dispose of a limit of words within it, chapter by chapter or section by section. And it is a matter of elementary kindness to yourself that you should know where you are, and what (at any given moment of authorship) you are attempting to do. One cannot sit down to write a thesis or a book. But one might, in practice, sit down to write Chapter Three.

Once the contents are clear, however provisionally, and in numbered sections, it is possible to attack the problem of how to marshal data. Some researchers prefer notebooks, some prefer slips of paper slid into folders and envelopes – and some like cards. A notebook has the virtue of slipping easily into the pocket when you go to a library; and it can even be scribbled in while waiting for the bus, or in even odder places. This may be called Hobbes's Way, since we know from John Aubrey's *Brief Lives* that Hobbes used it during the English Civil War when he was living in Paris and writing *Leviathan* (1651). His example is still highly instructive.

> The manner of writing of which book, he told me, was thus. He walked much and contemplated, and he had in the head of his staff a pen and ink-horn, carried always a notebook in his pocket; and as soon as a thought darted, he presently entered it into his book, or otherwise he might perhaps have lost it.

'Presently' means at once and without hesitation – a vital reminder that what an author leaves to memory, memory may as easily discard. Whatever is thought, if it was worth thinking, must be written down at once. But Hobbes's Way also offers an object-lesson in arrangement, or more strictly in what would nowadays be called data-processing:

He had drawn the design of the book into chapters etc, so he knew whereabout it would come in. Thus that book was made.

In other words, *Leviathan* owes its disciplined design and concentrated style to a technique of preparation reminiscent of the way molluscs build coral reefs – by a building process continuous over a wide area rather than in a single trajectory. And the more earnestly one considers such a mighty work of mind, the clearer it seems that such a book could *only* have been composed in some such way – barring the improbable accident of a memory more retentive than even the philosopher Hobbes is likely to have possessed. No notebook, no *Leviathan*.

Modern authors have a technical advantage over the seventeenth century in fountain-pens and biros; and Hobbes's ingenious expedient of building an ink-well into the top of his walking-stick, in the 1640s, need not detain them beyond a brief smile. Nor should the seeming inflexibility of a notebook – as opposed to cards or slips – deter: that inflexibility can easily be overestimated. A notebook is pocketable, for one thing; it does not (like cards or slips) disarrange itself; it allows for interpolations; and if Hobbes's Way is understood in its profundity, and chapter-headings are placed early at the heads of pages, then the notebook can itself become the organizing principle of the finished work. Once the notebook habit is acquired, the whole of life feels different forever after.

When the act of linear composition begins, in that case, the chief problem of arrangement has already been solved, in whole or in large part. The arrangement of chapters is by then essentially complete; the 'heads of the argument' (as Dryden called them) are already there, at least in provisional form; and quotations and other evidences garnered from reading in libraries are already deposited where they are likely to be needed. Every detail is placed 'whereabout it would come in', as Aubrey puts it. This is a well tried system that works, and for some kinds of scholarly writing it is doubtful if anything else does.

C. S. Lewis once showed a colleague the battered notebook from which he was writing his last scholarly book, *The Discarded Image* (1964), a composite study of man's idea of the universe before it was discarded by the scientific revolution of the seventeenth century. He had been lecturing from the notebook for some years, and had laid it out in Hobbes's Way, with headings for chapters and sub-chapters like 'The Earth', 'Beasts', 'The Human Soul' and 'The Seven Liberal Arts'. Lewis's argumentative heads or titles were placed on the right-hand side of the page, numbered and lettered in sequence:

V. The Heavens
   A The Parts of the Universe
   B Their Operations
   C Their Inhabitants

and opposite, on the left-hand side, were accumulated over the years quotations from many sources – ancient, medieval, Renaissance and even seventeenth century – each quotation illustrative of the argument on the opposite page. The notebook may have cost no more than a shilling, and its covers were battered and almost fallen apart from long use. But as with Hobbes's *Leviathan*, so with Lewis's briefer and far more modest exercise in intellectual debate; and once the simple principle has been explained, it is instantly apparent that such a book could hardly have been written in any other fashion.

Hobbes's Way has further practical advantages. One is that it defers most awkward problems of style, or *elocutio*, to a later stage. One can dash off a note on its appropriate page, 'whereabout it would come in', without a moment's stylistic constraint – happy in the perfect confidence that it can be radically rewritten later. And since arrangement or *dispositio* is usually the hardest part of scholarly composition – the most difficult part of writing a thesis is always the writing of it – there is every merit in lightening the burden of composition by pushing its graver problems to either side, into *inventio* and *elocutio*. All professionals know that. Evelyn Waugh once remarked in a radio interview that he hated writing, as many professional writers do, and was asked if that was because he hated sitting at a desk. 'No,' he said, 'it's having to think.'

In scholarly composition, however, like Hobbes's or Lewis's, it is possible to have done one's thinking, or most of it, before one writes – even though writing is always likely to demonstrate that there is more thinking still to be done. A notebook can solve that problem, or at least mitigate it. It is not difficult to have something to say: everyone has something to say. And saying it, when it comes to the point, can be easier than one thinks, since the thesis-writer is already trained to write sentences and paragraphs. His real difficulty is seeing where it will come in.

Another advantage in Hobbes's Way is that it ensures that prose is broken up. And it is essential that scholarly prose should be broken up. A thesis is not like thick soup: it is more like a well-arranged salad. And any first draft written without the early benefit of ordered notes is commonly too unwieldy. It is not just written in too many words. It is internally too long, so to speak: its sentences, its paragraphs, its chapters and sections are individually too long. Revision is commonly a search for shorter units: over-long sentences are broken up into shorter, and over-long sections are divided and then sub-divided, with headings to signpost the way.

Revision, in such cases, is a dissective act. It is rather like slicing an apple with a knife – first into halves, then into quarters, and then into still smaller divisions. And argumentative prose needs to be sliced. Nothing is more initially dispiriting to the reader of a scholarly book, article or thesis than the spectacle of heavy lumps of undivided prose. It dispirits even before any attempt to read it has been made. And that is a further reason why the division into chapters or sections should be conceived of early, and why chapter-headings reflecting a table of contents can guide the movement of prose as efficiently as a rush-hour traffic-cop. Even numbered sections without titles – some simple roman numerals, perhaps, such as I/II/III. . . – are easily better than nothing.

A good thesis, however it was conceived and drafted, must always end as a lucid arrangement of visibly distinct parts.

CHAPTER SEVEN
The writing bloc

Nobody has suffered more from low spirits than I have done – so I feel for you.

1st. Live as well as you dare.

2nd. Go into the shower-bath with a small quantity of water at a temperature low enough to give you a slight sensation of cold, 75° or 80°.

3rd. Amusing books.

4th. Short views of human life – not further than dinner or tea.

5th. Be as busy as you can.

6th. See as much as you can of those friends who respect and like you.

7th. And of those acquaintances who amuse you.

8th. Make no secret of low spirits to your friends, but talk of them freely – they are always worse for dignified concealment.

9th. Attend to the effects tea and coffee produce upon you.

10th. Compare your lot with that of other people.

11th. Don't expect too much from human life – a sorry business at the best.

12th. Avoid poetry, dramatic representations (except comedy), music, serious novels, melancholy sentimental people, and everything likely to excite feeling or emotion not ending in active benevolence.

13th. Do good, and endeavour to please everybody of every degree.

14th. Be as much as you can in the open air without fatigue.

15th. Make the room where you commonly sit gay and pleasant.

16th. Struggle by little and little against idleness.

17th. Don't be too severe upon yourself, or underrate yourself, but do yourself justice.

18th. Keep good blazing fires.

19th. Be firm and constant in the exercise of rational religion.

    Sydney Smith, letter to Lady Georgiana Morpeth (16 February 1820)

Henry James . . . counselled me: 'It's a great honour to be allowed to dream even that we may find a chance to produce a little life that is exempt from the law of extinction – not at the mercy of accident. Live your life, and stick to your table. Be a patient woman and a ferocious artist, and try to combine that mildness and that firmness. Nothing has helped me really but Time, and friendly response.'

Olivia Garnett, in The Legend of the Master, compiled by Simon
Nowell-Smith (1947)

The little girl had the makings of a poet in her who, being told to be sure of her meaning before she spoke, said: 'How can I know what I think till I see what I say?'

Graham Wallas, The Art of Thought (1926)

Why not write in the morning?

Unfortunately in my case there is never very much of the morning, and it is curious that although I do not despise people who go to bed earlier than I, almost everyone is impatient with me for not getting up. I may be working in bed on a wet morning, and they have nothing to do; yet they cannot conceal their feelings of superiority and ill will.

But between the dissipated, bedridden morning and the dangerous night fall the cicada hours of afternoon, so pregnant in their tedium; and these I now have free for the problem that is obsessing me.

Cyril Connolly, Enemies of Promise (1938) ch. 1

It is easy to write, hard only to write well.

That is where the writing bloc classically begins. Authors – and especially young authors – often suffer from a writing bloc or 'white-paper phobia'; and their suffering arises from the unspoken thought that, if they are to write at all, they must write well. And so, without meaning to do so, they forbid themselves to write – and then worry that they cannot. They are classically self-inhibited.

This chapter offers advice about how to contend with such inhibitions and free oneself of them. It is about how to lose the fear of writing, or of thinking oneself unable to write. The world, after all, is full of people who say they want to write, but who mean no more than that they want to have written. 'Says he wants to be a poet,' T. S. Eliot once remarked scornfully of a young man who had just been to see him. 'Didn't say anything about wanting to write poems.'

The first step is to recall that writing is a process and not a single act, and that there is no reasonable presumption that any single sentence should ever come right in its first draft. It may happen to do so; but it is not a natural expectation. Robert Graves spoke in old age of revising a poem up to twenty times, on occasion, and of foreseeing that process as he first drafted it; and Graham Greene, who regards himself as a perfectionist only when he writes, has described in an interview, *The Other Man* (1983), how after sixty years of effort, writing remains for him an act of repeated self-revision:

> I aim to be content with what I produce. It's an aim I never achieve, but I go over my work word by word, time and time again, so as to be as little dissatisfied as possible . . . A writer has to be his own judge . . . The harshest judgements should be his own (p. 121).

There is nothing discreditable, then, about a bad first draft. The life of an author is mostly a matter of pushing words about on the page – altering, reordering, adding, deleting, refining. And if an accomplished professional can do no better than that after half a century of daily experience, then it is not in nature that the beginner should do any better, and not reasonable that he should expect it.

The thought is liberating, rightly considered. It means that the first step towards defeating the bloc, to put it bluntly, is to lower standards. Nothing need come out right the first time. Every sentence – every phrase, perhaps – is subject to revision, and perhaps to multiple revision. At that early stage, nothing commits. 'I just put down any sort of rubbish,' a celebrated critic once remarked about his first attempts. And putting down rubbish is good advice; even if not all teachers, fearful of misconstruction, have the audacity to give it. But the truth is that once a sentence is lying on the page, it is often shatteringly clear what is right and what is wrong with it. Put it down, and go on putting more of it down. Everything can be mended later.

Writing a thesis starts with writing, not with preparing to write. You may feel you are not ready to start writing, and may even invoke Hobbes's Way with a notebook as an excuse. But Hobbes's notebook was *written*, though not (it seems safe to assume) written in anything like its final form. And feeling unready is no excuse at all. In scholarship one is never ready, since there is always something more one could sensibly read. All scholarship, strictly speaking, is at first written by the unprepared, or at least by the under-prepared.

That principle, uncomfortable and deflating as it sounds, is a logically necessary one – at least so far as first drafts are concerned. The decisive moment comes when you notice that it is so, and necessarily so, and draw a natural conclusion from that bitter and sceptical truth. Since you are never ready to write, you start writing before you are ready. 'Collecting materials' is the shabbiest of all excuses here, and if you are candid it will not fool even yourself. No committee, certainly, and no supervisor is likely to be impressed by the claim that the research has been done and only needs to be 'written up'. *No* research has been done, in any sense that counts, until writing has been done; and those who speak of 'writing up' rather than writing betray a total ignorance of what they are at.

Sketch a draft table of contents at first meeting with the supervisor; and if the supervisor is realistic, he may decline to see you again without the text of at least one chapter or section, however inchoate. Writing starts at once. If it does not start at once, then the impulse can turn dead or (what is worse) sour; and the harder you concentrate, the harder it will become, like a nervous swimmer hesitating to take the plunge. Coleridge, that classic hesitator who in the event finished more works than many of his severer critics, invitingly entitled the eleventh chapter of his *Biographia Literaria* (1817) 'An affectionate exhortation to those who in early life feel themselves disposed to become authors', remarking that an impulse to write can be self-defeating in its very intensity, and that in authorship, as in life, one can achieve more if one expects less:

> Motives by excess reverse their very nature, and instead of exciting, stun and stupefy the mind.

Many young authors, as Coleridge knew from experience, spend hours in the agonies of self-stupefaction when they ought to be scribbling bad sentences: sentences which, once written, could easily be trimmed, refined and rendered acceptable or something more. The *Biographia* itself, which burst out of Coleridge during the summer of 1815 in a mood of dour self-reproach after some fifteen years of hesitation, shows what quick drafting can achieve, even if by modern scholarly standards it is woefully wayward in argument and under-revised in style.

Quick drafting suggests a mood of 'relaxation, and one totally foreign to self-importance. That mood can be difficult to achieve, to the extent that an author thinks highly of himself, or imagines that others think highly of him. In that fearful expectation, he can tense himself into a bloc, instead of relaxing into an easy and uncritical flow. One should try at such moments to think little or nothing of oneself: this is a moment for conscious and deliberate self-humiliation. If it helps to call a first draft something as derisive and dismissive as 'rubbishing it out', then call it that. Some writers have been known to murmur to themselves 'Garbage, garbage' as they draft; and T. S. Eliot, in the same spirit, once remarked to Lawrence

Durrell: 'I always try to make the whole business seem as unimportant as I can' (*Atlantic Monthly* May 1965).

There are more specific devices that can help. If writing letters to friends is easy, as many of us find, then pretend to write a letter. There are letter-novels, after all: so why not a letter-thesis, with the usual forms like 'Dear X' eventually to be chopped off? One best-selling author, knowing himself a hapless victim to white-paper phobia, defeated it by going out and buying himself a quire of green. And it helps to think of a thesis less in terms of the whole than as an assembly of morsels – the draft table of contents reminding you where the morsel will eventually be. Take 'short views of human life,' the Reverend Sydney Smith once advised a friend, in a letter devoted to the unusual topic of happiness – 'not further than dinner or tea' (16 Febuary 1820). Short views can be good for a writer's happiness too. And if a morsel is all you attempt, then it can be scribbled at once, even in a crowded room or on a train or bus. Writing is not always performed alone at a desk; and a pocket note-book means that the best notions, if they come unawares, can be memorialized at once.

Once a single word is on the page, there is a narrowing set of possibilities as to what the second word can be; and the possibilities for the third are narrower still. And with every sentence and paragraph that is written, similarly, the next grows easier. That is why composition needs to be loosened into the freedom of quick-running mental association. Never, at first draft, interrupt that flow to confirm a fact, verify a quotation or ascertain a reference: all that may be filled in later, in revision; and always try to stop, if stop you must, at a point where it is easy to go on – with a simple piece of transcription, perhaps – so that you resume without anxiety or delay.

Even rational objections may be rationally postponed. 'It is a bad thing,' Schiller once wrote to a young poet in December 1788,

> and detrimental to the creative work of mind, if Reason makes too
> close an examination of ideas as they pour in at the very gateway. A
> thought may seem very trivial or fantastic; but it can be made
> important by another thought that comes after it, and may form an
> effective link. Reason must relax its hold on the gates, and let ideas
> rush in pell-mell . . . You critics complain of infertility, because you
> reject too soon and discriminate too severely.

The letter understandably appealed to Sigmund Freud, who quoted it with lively approval in his *Interpretation of Dreams* (1900). What starts as garbage ends as something else; and all formal edifices, it is good to remember, even the most severely classical, began as rough blocks. White-paper phobia is conquered, as Schiller and Freud saw, by conquering one's natural or over-educated disdain for the indiscriminate rubbish of mind. If it is a mind at all, then what it holds is not entirely rubbish. And it is out of what it holds, rubbish or not – and only there – that mind can create at all.

The rewards of rubbish are considerable. An early draft, once down on the page, can be more engrossing than the best prose in the world. That is not because it is better than most prose, or as good. (It is usually much worse.) It engrosses because, bad as it is, it is yours, and yours to change. It is now in that most fascinating of all artistic states – a state of becoming. And that can easily excite more than any state of perfected completion. In a picture-gallery, for similar reasons, visitors will congregate around a student copying a great master, and pay far closer and longer analytical attention to his draft or daub than to the finished work of a great hand. That is because the masterpiece is completed, or as complete as it will ever be. The copy, poor as it may be, is not.

Study the effects upon yourself of the hour of the day. There are day-birds and night-birds – early writers and late. You can then take a crucial decision on what part of the day you will set aside for writing, and build the rest of the day around that focus of routine. Joseph Conrad trained himself to sit at his desk every day at a given hour, regardless of whether he had anything in his mind to write or not. But it is worth noting again that no one need work at a desk at all, unless he is typing, and that a first draft can be achieved in the most comfortable chair that there is. (A sofa can be even better, since it gives spaces to spread papers.) Conrad might have been easier on himself, what is more, if he had conceived of his first sentence for the day before sitting down at all.

If it works for you, then it works. Goethe used to say that he could only write if he was uncomfortable, and Virginia Woolf for a time wrote standing at a lectern; but nobody need think of such cases as anything more than curious. Only one general proposition may be true here: the earlier in the day, the better. That can be the hardest time of all to write, or even to be up, in the sense of being the hardest time to start. But anyone who creates for himself a routine of starting every day with writing, and that very early, will have discovered the most powerful cure for the writing bloc that there is. The bloc will not just vanish, in his fortunate case, but go into reverse: filled with a sense of achievement for the remaining hours of the day, and pleasurably obsessed with the happy task of making sentences and paragraphs, he will return to it at every moment he is free to return. The whole world, as he knows it, will turn into his essay or his book. Such premature authors have been known to put a completed thesis into a drawer, waiting till it is time to submit it.

Authorship has advantages over other kinds of utterance, such as conversation, and it is as well to recognize and exploit them. One is that a writer can cast into final and telling form what, in his ordinary speech, may have been no more than a fumbling attempt. An author can be helped, then, by an inadequate personality; and it is out of that sense of inadequacy that authors, like actors, are sometimes born. Literature can easily be a sort of extended *esprit de l'escalier*: something you thought of too late to say at the time, but are overwhelmingly eager to say now that you have belatedly thought of it. It can help to be unwitty. That is a good reason for discussing your thoughts with anyone who will listen, whether inside the subject or out. No need for concern, certainly, if mind moves slowly and social graces are deficient. Writing may ultimately be all the better for both.

Perhaps the best counter of all to a writing bloc, and one only rarely and preciously achieved, is anger. That is how letters to newspaper-editors are commonly written, and the instinct is sound even where the style and sentiment are not. Authors seldom write so fast or so well as when they are angry – with others, or with themselves. 'Is it as bad as that?' a sister asks sympathetically, when the hero of Evelyn Waugh's *Put Out More Flags* (1942) tells her he has a good mind to write a book about the war. A thesis, like a letter or a book, may well be embarked on because things are indeed as bad as that: a question shamefully neglected or misunderstood, an author scandalously under- or over-rated, a problem ignored. An anti-papal historian once remarked that he wrote because he was read and resented in the Vatican; and it hardly matters whether he was or not, since it was only in that sublime confidence of giving annoyance that he wrote at all. To be angry, for an author, is to be in luck.

CHAPTER EIGHT
Discovery

Not long ago, Sir Peter Medawar remarked that when the momentous DNA discoveries were being made, there were plenty of people in the English faculties of universities quite as clever as [Francis] Crick and [James] Watson. But Crick and Watson had something to be clever about . . . No creative upheaval like the Modernist movement of the earlier part of this century has come about to make us re-draw the map of literary history. So one has had the sad spectacle of many trim and high-powered intellectual machines with their wheels spinning vainly in the air.

Naturally this situation could not be allowed to continue: and there were indeed plenty of people clever enough to do something about it. If no problems offer themselves, problems can be invented. If mowing the lawn with the mowing machine has become too easy, you can always try doing it with the vacuum-cleaner. Ancillary disciplines can be brought in and applied to questions for which they were not intended. A system devised for the analysis of Russian folk-tales can be adapted to the later novels of Henry James. The microscopic machinery of phonemic analysis can be blown up to the macroscopic scale, and used to examine the structure of narrative. And endless fascinating variations can be discovered in practically anything, by applying what the French (but nobody else) can recognise as psychoanalysis.

And so we have had Saussurian and Jakobsonian linguistics, Lévi-Straussian structuralism, Barthesian structuralism, post-structuralism, Derrida, de Man, deconstruction. A Marxist tincture has always been acceptable to the French *avant-garde*: so, dutifully, in England and the United States, the ashes of Thirties Marxism were rekindled to a subfusc glow. And so one problem was solved. Now there was plenty to be clever about.

Graham Hough, *London Review of Books* (17 October 1985)

A thesis unfolds the results of research.

Research by its nature seeks to reveal something new: not just new to you, but new absolutely. It tells the world something it did not know; and something which, as its author hopes and believes, it ought to know. It is not primarily an exercise in self-exploration, or a declaration of sincerity, or even a means of study, though all such matters can arise in the course of things. A thesis is based on a discovery, and its prime aim is to declare it.

Discovery is only likely to be achieved by those who think there is something to be discovered, and whose minds are trained to discover it. Those who imagine that all the subjects that count have already been provided for, in scholarly terms, are not merely mistaken about the state of scholarship: their mistake is of a self-destructive kind that deeply disqualifies them for research. As a premise, it is totally disabling; and the diluted form of that premise – that only trivia remain to be dealt with – is only a little better. Discovery only happens to those who seek it out; and they will only seek it out if they are convinced that new and momentous knowledge is there to be found.

Research usually springs from a conviction, whether certain or otherwise, that something unnoticed is likely to be true. If the world is indeed round, then it must be possible to reach China by sailing west as well as east. It is at that sublime moment that the joy of the chase is justly yours. That sense of joy, or prospective joy, amply needs to be there. Consultants such as teachers and librarians can be generous with advice, but they cannot reasonably be asked to supply an enthusiasm that you lack. If they take fire from your idea, then the fire must first be yours. An element of fanaticism, however decorously contained, is appropriate to the occasion. If you do not believe in your own idea, no one else will. This is not a moment to be modest or tentative. It is your idea that is about to be tested; it is your advocacy that will make it strong enough, and flexible enough, to survive the doubts and fears of others.

Never ask another, then, to supply an enthusiasm that you lack. The supervisor acts as a brake here, not as a spur. It is entirely natural that he should have doubts, and put them. That is what he is for. Better to hear them now, surely, than later: in fact the earlier they are heard and sifted, the better.

It is at this point that works of reference will most naturally be appealed to. 'Hadn't you better look in X first?' may be the first warning note to be heard, where X refers to a work you should already have consulted. Monographs and reference-books exist unashamedly to make one appear more learned than one is. But it is by claiming to be that that scholars are made, and scholarship richly illustrates the existentialist principle that you become the thing that you do. Many a researcher has consulted such books, under advice, as no more than a whimsical concession to the conscientious doubts or fears of others – only to discover that scholarship is fascinating as well as prudent, seductive as well as dry, and magnetic in its power to create obsessions that last a lifetime.

Not everyone that yields to that obsession emerges unscathed, or at all: the processes of scholarship can take possession of minds forever. And a great library, especially in its battery of reference-books, can suddenly look like a great orchestra where the researcher, like a maestro, conducts. The knowledge of how libraries work can confer a sense of the potency of creative scholarship on its acolytes: an instant awareness that there are, after all, things to discover, and in a non-trivial sense that professionally counts. Such things may perhaps be known already, in the sense of having found their way into print. But they have not been used in the context of one's own subject, for all that, or seen to have the significance that they have, or understood for what in truth they are.

A beginner is allowed to avow ignorance of the great scholarly aids – dictionaries, encyclopaedias, printed library catalogues and the like. But not for long. No one has to remain a beginner, and there is a point beyond which ignorance ceases to look engaging and starts to look crass. The Renaissance researcher who in his last year of research asked his supervisor what the letters '*STC*' meant, when followed by a number, is still spoken of in academe with just derision. (*STC* is explained below.) No one need go to London, for instance, to discover if the British Library has a book or periodical: it has published its catalogue in many volumes – commonly known as *BLC* – and many libraries possess it. So has the Bibliothèque Nationale in Paris; and so has the Library of Congress in Washington: or rather, the *National Union Catalog* which began to be issued in printed volumes in 1968 is based on that library and on other public libraries in the United States and Canada, listing locations of copies in the public collections of North America. And such works are not only useful to world-travellers. It can be helpful to know that a book or an edition exists, even if one cannot immediately consult it, and even if one can never consult it. Besides, copies can sometimes be obtained through inter-library loans or xerox copies.

Original discovery can be made from entirely unoriginal sources, just as in cooking an original recipe can be made from entirely familiar ingredients. Even the middle-aged, like William Empson when he came to write *The Structure of Complex Words* (1951), some-times belatedly notice that original research can be based on a reference-book as familiar as the *Oxford English Dictionary*, commonly known as *OED*, which began to appear as the *New English Dictionary* (*NED*) in 1888: laid out on historical principles, and documented with literary examples, it proffers a vast data-bank of critical information, much of it still totally unused by literary and intellectual historians, on richly significant words like 'wit' and 'nature'. One sometimes needs to be middle-aged to realise that prime evidence can be as publicly available as this and still untapped. Much of *OED*, from the historian's viewpoint, looks like a rusting armoury that has never been taken from the wall.

Such sources are not hard to find, and a mere glance around the reading room of an academic library will sometimes find them. The chief literary bibliographies of English are commonly known as *New CBEL* and *BAL*. The first, or the *New Cambridge Bibliography of English Literature*, edited by George Watson and Ian Willison, lists the literature of the British Isles from its Anglo-Saxon beginnings down to such authors as were established by 1950, with secondary material; the second, or *Bibliography of American Literature*, was largely edited by Jacob Blanck, and it lists American authors alphabetically and without secondary material.

For the earlier periods of English, at least, English is by now provided for by reference-books of unexampled richness. All books published in the British Isles between Caxton in the 1470s and the year 1640, regardless of language, are listed with locations of copies on both sides of the Atlantic in *Short-Title Catalogue 1475–1640*, universally known as *STC*, of which a revised edition has appeared; its sequel, commonly known as *Wing* after the name of its first editor, and also under revision, lists all English books for the ensuing sixty years, or 1641–1700; and vast supplements on the eighteenth and even nineteenth centuries, necessarily less full and less reliable, are already under way. All pre-1700 English books, whether *STC* or *Wing*, are now available on microfilm published by University Microfilms Inc, and some libraries stock readable enlargements of microfilm by Copyflo. Many learned libraries, what is more, maintain marked copies of *STC* and *Wing* in their reading rooms, interleaved and corrected with pencilled notes on local holdings. In principle, then, it is possible to find the location of any English book published before 1700 and even afterwards, anywhere in the world in public collections. No other modern literature is blessed with aids of such abundance and skill; though Europe as a whole has an *STC* of sixteenth-century books entitled *Index Aureliensis*, published in Germany.

Writing a thesis

For more special tastes, more special aids exist. Early eighteenth-century English poetry, for example, has David Foxon's *English Verse 1701–50*, listing all separately printed poems from the half-century of Pope and Swift, and its index enables a reader to consult topics as well as authors. Foxon also lists locations of copies – an invaluable addition, since some of these works survive only in rare or even unique copies. With such a book to hand, the difficulty is not in making discoveries but in avoiding them. J. M. Kuist's *Nichols File of the Gentleman's Magazine* lists author-attributions from 1731 to the 1860s. And the enormous, untapped riches of nineteenth-century periodical literature are now being mapped by Walter Houghton's *Wellesley Index to Victorian Periodicals 1824–1900*, which attempts to pierce the anonymity of articles in forty-eight periodicals of the age, published in a century when most periodical articles and book reviews were anonymous; and by the four-volume *British Literary Magazines*, edited by Alvin Sullivan, which describes some four hundred journals since 1698, period by period – volume 3, for example, is devoted to 1837–1913 – with notes on locations of full or partial runs and on secondary sources, but no itemized contents. For the twentieth century there is an eight-volume *Comprehensive Index to English-Language Little Magazines 1890–1970*, edited by Marion Sader, an alphabetical author-index of non-commercial reviews like *Agenda* and *Poetry (Chicago)*.

For theatre, especially recent theatre, there are few books that carry enquiry much beyond the earliest stage, if the search is for evidences of performances and of original reviews. But the British Theatre Association (Regents College, Inner Circle, Regents Park, London NW1) preserves in its library and for the use of members stage year-books listing theatrical performances with cast-details, indexing all performances reviewed in the *Times*, the *Financial Times* and the *Daily Telegraph*. To join such a society is to open the door to endless and covetable research into the creative life of modern London theatre, and to gain access to otherwise unattainable material.

Some reference-books are divertingly specialist. There is a German guide to European emblem-literature, for example – Henkel and Schöne's *Emblemata: Handbuch zur Sinnbildkunst des 16. und 17. Jahrhunderts*; it lacks an author-index, and the theme-index is in German only, the body of the text being in the original languages. Other specialist aids are unpublished, and likely to remain so, though available to serious enquiries preceded by a letter. The Warburg Institute, for example, in Woburn Square, London WC1, has a photo-file of the great themes of Western art, mainly from paintings

48

of the late Middle Ages and early modern period, including the Greek and Latin myths and all the chapters of the Bible from Genesis to Revelation; and the Courtauld Institute, in Portman Square, London W1, has a photo-file ordered not by theme but by artist. For actualities, the Radio Times Hulton Picture Library (BBC Publications, 35 Marylebone High St, London W1) has over six million photos ranging from prehistoric cave paintings to recent events, charging a fee for their use.

Other reference-books are the reverse of specialist. They exist, that is to say, to be used by non-specialists seeking a clear and succinct statement of some matter where they are rightly content to remain amateurs. That is what general encyclopaedias do; and recent instances like Paul Edwards's *Encyclopaedia of Philosophy*, or *Everyman's Dictionary of Economics* edited by Arthur Seldon and F. G. Pennance, assume no special knowledge and give the gist of a problem in concise form. No shame attaches to asking librarians for such books: it is not like the literary researcher who was rightly embarrassed to have to ask what *STC* means. One simply enquires for a reference-book about philosophy or economics.

For manuscripts, where original discovery is hard to avoid, there are published catalogues of large library holdings such as the British Library, the Bodleian, the New York Public Library and the Folger Library in Washington, as well as of smaller college collections like M. R. James's volumes on Cambridge colleges or R. A. B. Mynors's *Catalogue of the Manuscripts of Balliol College, Oxford* (1963). For historical manuscripts, the best place to start can be the *Guide to the Contents of the Public Records Office* in three volumes (1963–68) or, for the more courageous, the vast publications of the Historical Manuscripts Commission, which in 1945 set up a National Register of Archives, including those in private hands (Quality House, Quality Court, Chancery Lane, London WC2). The riches of the PRO are broadly indicated by V. H. Galbraith's *Introduction to the Use of Public Records* (1934, revised 1952); and of parish records by W. E. Tate, *The Parish Chest* (1946, revised 1969), which includes a glossary of terms on parochial administration.

The great manuscript catalogues, as one might expect, are exact in proportion as they refer to early periods; and perhaps the most exact of all, for English literature, is N. R. Ker's *Catalogue of Manuscripts Containing Anglo-Saxon* (1957). The modern period is now being opened with Peter Beal's *Index of English Literary Manuscripts*, which began to appear in 1980 with volumes devoted to its earliest period, which is 1450–1625; it is arranged alphabetically author by author, with details about locations as well as the publication of manuscripts, where they exist, and of facsimiles. It will eventually include eighteenth- and nineteenth-century English authors, ending around 1900. And for North America there is the vast and composite *National Union Catalog of Manuscript Collections*, which lists holdings in the United States under authors.

A manuscript, even a highly important manuscript, may be known and yet unused, so that discovery here can easily mean reporting on something already listed and already available. It is astonishing how seldom even the greatest and most famous of manuscripts are visited by the residents of towns where they have lain for years and even centuries, even when they are university towns – so much so that librarians often look surprised when asked for them, usually by a visiting Japanese. Odd as it must seem, manuscripts can be well known and yet simply ignored in research; rash to assume, then, that because a manuscript is well known it is not worth consulting. And their use can confer a distinction on a thesis like no other. The style of a thesis may be plodding, its critical perceptions commonplace – but if its author took the adventurous step of looking at a manuscript and telling what was in it, the prize for initiative can easily outweigh all the blame that can attach to other deficiencies. There is no advantage so unimpeachable in a thesis as the simple truth that it has used materials of consequence that have not previously been used.

It is widely known that wills proved in England and Wales are filed at the Probate Registry, Somerset House, London WC2, where they can be inspected for a small fee. They may contain information about the career, acquaintanceship and properties of an historical figure, and of a sort untapped by historical scholarship; and there is a brief introduction in B. G. Bouwens's *Wills and their Whereabouts* (1939, revised 1963). The riches of county archives are more impressively neglected. If your author was born in, or long resident in, a given county, all you then need to know is the name of the county town. Write, in that case, to the County Archivist at its town hall – no further address is usually necessary – explaining your needs in detail: the exact date of birth, marriage or death of an author, for example, or other historical figure, and whatever other factual problems remain to be solved. County archivists are usually happy to receive and answer such letters, and they often possess or have access to documents unknown to the world of scholarship and utterly unlisted outside their own archives. Such help, which should be conscientiously acknowledged in a preface, can turn an amateur thesis into a professional treatise at a stroke.

Amazing how much original research can be performed for the price of a postage-stamp.

CHAPTER NINE
Interviews

It may be objected by some persons, as it has been by one of my
friends, that he who has the power of thus exhibiting an exact
transcript of conversations is not a desirable member of society . . .

On the other hand, how useful is such a faculty, if well exercised!
To it we owe all those interesting apothegms and memorabilia of the
Ancients which Plutarch, Xenophon and Valerius Maximus have
transmitted to us. To it we owe all those instructive and entertaining
collections which the French have made under the title of *Ana*, affixed
to some celebrated name. To it we owe the *Table-talk* of Selden, the
Conversation between Ben Jonson and Drummond of Hawthornden,
Spence's *Anecdotes* of Pope, and other valuable remains in our own
language. How delighted should we have been, if thus introduced into
the company of Shakespeare and of Dryden, of whom we know
scarcely any thing but their admirable writings! What pleasure would it
have given us to have known their petty habits, their characteristic
manners, their modes of composition, and their genuine opinion of
preceding writers and of their contemporaries!

All these are now irrevocably lost. Considering how many of the
strongest and most brilliant effusions of exalted intellect must have
perished, how much is it to be regretted that all men of distinguished
wisdom and wit have not been attended by friends of taste enough to
relish, and abilities enough to register, their conversation!

James Boswell, *Journal of a Tour to the Hebrides* (1785)

Research can be done through books, as everyone knows; and, as
only some know, it can be done by letters. It can also be performed
through conversation.

There are two ways by which conversation can form the basis of
research. In the first, it can be the chief source of evidence, if the
topic is a recent one like the policy of a recent government or the
career of a twentieth-century author. A. J. A. Symons wrote *The*

Quest for Corvo (1934), his life of Frederick Rolfe, by talking to those who remembered Rolfe as well as by using letters and other surviving documents. If the author is still alive, it seems a pity not to meet him; if only recently dead, a pity not to meet those who still remember him.

The second way to use conversation is to extend and enrich a knowledge possessed – confirming and revising an understanding already, in some degree, enjoyed. Conversation can 'give a feel' of something, even if it tells you nothing you did not already know. There is even an advantage, well known to journalists, of being there – even if one meets no one there who remembers the events in question. One cannot research on Proust without having seen Paris; it may be unclear why not, but everyone can perceive it is so. It would be rather like expecting to learn to ride a bike by reading a set of directions.

An acquaintance pursued in the interests of research usually begins with a letter to a famous being; and it is as well to take stock of what such a letter, from a stranger, should most promisingly contain, and how it should be phrased. The problem is not confined to one of tone. Some authors and retired public figures positively enjoy the thought of being researched, since they have an entirely proper and natural interest in their standing and future fame in the world. Far fewer, however, relish the thought of being the subject of a graduate or undergraduate essay where, as they may easily imagine, a beginner might commit all sorts of amateurish errors and achieve nothing more, in the end, than a typescript read by one or two examiners. Jean-Paul Sartre, it is said, was easy to meet in Paris, unless he knew you were a graduate student. And this is where the first practical difficulty with research interviews begins.

At its bluntest, the difficulty is one of honesty. A student can hardly deny he is that; and he can hardly deny, if pressed, that he is seeking an advantage over other candidates in gaining access to a famous source. But the dilemma is not absolute. Many an author, though chary of the academic thesis, may actively encourage research into himself if he believes it will emerge, at a later stage, as something more than that. Some think themselves undervalued by the world, and perhaps for good reason; and the researcher, since he has chosen the topic, may easily think so too. Some, equally, think themselves misunderstood. Others, like Samuel Beckett, may adopt an attitude intermediate between refusal and full cooperation, as they are entitled to do – agreeing to meet a biographer and converse, but declining to answer all the questions put or to make any manuscripts available. The possibilities here are not confined to two, and a subject may converse without revealing all he knows. It is with that range of possibilities in mind that an initial letter, preferably addressed from an academic institution and on official writing-paper, may appeal to something more, and more reliable, than a sense of generosity.

A first letter may helpfully emphasize any one of these possibilities. It may suggest that the author is under-valued, or that his writings have been misunderstood. Such suggestions, which need to be sincere to count at all, may reasonably find a welcome. Many public figures feel that the world has missed the point they were trying to make, or part of it; and it is proper, in those circumstances, that they should seek to correct what they suppose an error in critical opinion. And the critic is seldom so well employed as when he reports, even without comment, what they have to say about such misunderstandings.

That is not to say that one is bound totally to accept everything one hears. A politician may be as mistaken about the significance of what he did or failed to do, an author about the significance of what he wrote, as any other being. That may be so through forgetfulness, through unconscious suppression, or by virtue of some self-excusing motive that animates most existences, literary or other. Prime evidence, or the horse's mouth, is not infallible evidence. There is no such thing as infallible evidence. But it is still evidence; and if it is unique to the thesis, then it can be a striking and even decisive element in its value.

Conversations are all too quickly forgotten. If the conversation occurs in an atmosphere too intimate for taking notes, like Boswell's conversations with Johnson, then it is highly prudent to write them down within hours of leaving, and preferably within minutes. One of the best of Victorian memoirs, Lord Stanhope's *Notes on Conversations with the Duke of Wellington 1831–51* (1886), was written down (as Stanhope explains in his preface) by dictation to his wife 'either on the same day, or at furthest the day after, the conversations which they record'; and Stanhope adds that he never noted anything 'when not quite sure of remembering it exactly'. The book is far less deliberately arranged than Boswell's *Johnson*, and looks all the more trustworthy for that reason; in fact it illustrates the supreme interest of raw and undoctored material, where evidence is set down for future use without fuss or excess of comment. It is frustrating to realise, in later years, how compelling a book one might have compiled simply by writing down the interesting things one has heard said every day of one's life.

Even unwritten assistance needs to be gratefully acknowledged – usually at the end of the preface, where other acknowledgements are made. In that case the extent of the debt to conversation, or to unpublished letters and other papers, needs to be clearly stated, and gratitude should be openly offered for permission to quote. Letters quoted at length or in their entirety may under copyright law require permission even in a thesis – whether from the author or, if he is deceased, from his literary executor; at least that can be true where theses are made available in libraries and qualify, for that reason, as publication. But copyright law allows reasonable quotation without permission, though not the quotation of whole works. Reported conversations normally require no permission to quote; but it is a matter of courtesy to assure oneself, by letter or by word of mouth, that no objection is to be raised.

CHAPTER TEN
Bad arguments

Our comments on life and affairs were bright and amusing, but brittle
– as I said of the conversation of [Bertrand] Russell and myself with
[D. H.] Lawrence – because there was no solid diagnosis of human
nature underlying them. Bertie in particular sustained simultaneously a
pair of opinions ludicrously incompatible. He held that in fact human
affairs were carried on after a most irrational fashion, but that the
remedy was quite simple and easy, since all we had to do was to carry
them on rationally.

> John Maynard Keynes, 'My early beliefs' (1938), in his *Two
> Memoirs* (1949)

Whereas no two propositions can be in themselves mutually
contradictory, there are many cases in which one and the same pair of
propositions are capable of being thought either that or the opposite,
according as the questions they were meant to answer are
reconstructed in one way or another.

For example, metaphysicians have been heard to say 'the world is
both one and many'; and critics have not been wanting who were
stupid enough to accuse them of contradicting themselves, on the
abstractly logical ground that 'the world is one' and 'the world is
many' are mutually contradictory propositions. A great deal of the
popular dislike of metaphysics is based on grounds of this sort, and is
ultimately due to critics who, as we say, did not know what the men
they criticized were talking about; that is, did not know what
questions their talk was intended to answer; but, with the ordinary
malevolence of the idle against the industrious, the ignorant against the
learned, the fool against the wise man, wished to have it believed that
they were talking nonsense.

> R. G. Collingwood, *An Autobiography* (1939) ch. 5

An argument is usually the prevailing pattern of a thesis; and
some arguments are better than others.

This chapter is about bad arguments, then, as they commonly appear in theses. It is not implacably hostile. Any argument, if lucidly presented as that, is likely to be better than none. It may be something of a compliment to an argument, for that reason, to call it bad, or indeed to call it anything. If it has risen to the level where it is worth refuting, then it is plainly worth something, and something better than most. It is better than mere fudge.

To call an argument bad is not, or not necessarily, to dismiss it; and to show in detail why it is bad is to take it in the highest spirit of seriousness that scholarship allows of. Scholarship thrives on argument – good, bad and indifferent. Indeed, it is a question whether, if we never had bad or indifferent arguments, we could have good ones at all.

This chapter, then, may be taken as measured (but never ecstatic) praise of argumentative weakness. In order to be believed by anybody, after all, a bad argument is always likely to contain a good deal of truth: it is commonly a good argument that has gone at least slightly off the rails. Quite right, for that reason, to take it seriously – especially if it has been widely believed – and quite right to be grateful for it. Like conversation, scholarly argument thrives on a dialectic, or contest, or to-and-fro of debate; and it is not in nature that everything said in a good conversation or a good scholarly debate should be cogent or true.

The dialectic of debate has been described by Plato in his *Republic* books vi–vii, and it is the way by which, as he saw, intellectual advance occurs. It is not cynical, then, to love bad arguments. What is cynical is to pretend to a view that everyone, in the end, knows to be false: that any argument is good if it is held with passionate sincerity. But the truth of an argument is independent of the sincerity, or cynicism, with which it is held. Our own age is littered with views which, like Nazism, were totally sincere and totally worthless; and such instances demonstrate to the hilt that an intellectual debate is only seriously that if it is prepared to analyse argument without regard to the sincerity or longevity of its belief, and to test its truth regardless of any intensity of conviction that may have been brought to it by the many or the few.

Such scepticism is exceptional. But then writing or examining a thesis is exceptional too. It is not in doubt that the study of the past or present of mankind – its institutions and its arts – can be uncritically performed, in a mildly appreciative way; and there are those who are content it should never be anything more. Some even insist on it. But those who read theses, like most of those who write them, can readily see two fatal objections to the merely appreciative view of history and the arts of man. One is that mere appreciation refuses to take the past at its word, content to trivialize it for the purposes of immediate and personal gratification. And the other is that bad arguments, if never exposed as bad, create a growing tolerance for more and more bad arguments – an affect that cannot deserve to be called educative.

If you can find some one to say you are wrong – preferably on an early draft – and why you are wrong, you have found a friend. A merely appreciative remark may imply that the draft has not been pondered or even read. One invites attack, and for good reason: conscious, as ever, that to attack a view is in no way to attack the author.

★ ★ ★

Some familiar types of bad argument may be conveniently set out in numbered order.

1. An argument cannot afford to be self-contradictory; for where two views contradict each other, at least one of them is wrong. If, as certain critical theorists of the 1960s supposed, we need a precise description of literature before knowing what it is, and if all language (being arbitrary) is non-descriptive, then it cannot be an objection to the state of criticism to say that we have no precise description of literature, or of anything else. Or again, if, as Marxists have believed, social conditioning always determines ideology, then the ideological convictions of Marx and Engels must have been so determined; and if it is an objection to the truth of a doctrine to say that it is so determined, then it is an objection to theirs. If, as extreme philosophical sceptics believe, all general propositions are false, then so is that, since it is a general proposition. If every intellectual enquiry requires an intellectual basis, then that view of intellectual enquiry, in its turn, requires such a basis, which in its turn would require another. No theory that seeks to be taken seriously can afford to represent an exception to itself. That is what self-contradiction means; and it rings a loud alarm-bell from the moment it is sniffed.

2. Familiar phrases can beg questions that need to be considered afresh, and it is out of such fresh reconsiderations that good theses can emerge. A phrase like 'Defoe's bourgeois ethic' or 'Victorian *laissez-faire*' makes assumptions that are only of value

if they have been examined and tested against evidence. It is not obvious that there ever was such a thing as a bourgeoisie in early eighteenth-century England, or that (if there was) it held the social views glibly attributed to it; or that any Victorian legislator ever believed in *laissez-faire*, or ever behaved as if he did. That certain nineteenth-century thinkers like Carlyle and Matthew Arnold believed that they did is nothing conclusive, as evidence: they could have been mistaken. No critic is an authority, then or now; no good critic has authorities. He exists to doubt. And it is when he doubts familiar and question-begging phrases that research often begins.

3. No claim is true or false because it can be shown to be an archetype or a stereotype. The historical existence of Jesus has been questioned on the ground that the Gospels reflect messianic cults familiar in the Middle East in ancient times. But so do many modern lives reflect familiar patterns or stereotypes, like Don Quixote or Don Juan: so much so that one might easily describe an acquaintance as quixotic or 'a bit of a Don Juan' without doubting his existence. People live conventions as well as write them: that is how conventions become that. The French letter-novel *Lettres portugaises* (1668) is now known to be a novel, and not (as was long supposed) a translated collection of genuine letters written to her lover by a Portuguese nun. But the fact that the style of these letters is highly conventional is not, of itself, a sufficient reason for thinking the book to be fictional. Many real letters are highly conventional; and conventions, for that matter, can be heartfelt. Dylan Thomas may well have lived the Wordsworthian idyll of 'Fern Hill' as a child before he ever thought of writing a poem about it, and before he had ever heard of Wordsworth.

4. Incompatibilities can be true in the sense that individuals can believe in both. Virginia Woolf was a pacifist, but profoundly regretted in 1936 that Britain could not give military help to the Spanish Republic. Anti-semites really do have Jews as their best friends, on occasion; but when they do, the fact is not a sufficient reason for doubting their anti-semitism. George Orwell's journalism in the 1940s could be highly collectivist: his last two fictions, *Animal Farm* and *Nineteen Eighty-Four*, are the reverse. Socialists claim to be anti-capitalist; and yet they often want the state, which is easily the biggest capitalist that there is, to be bigger still. And Conservatives often say they believe in

competitive private enterprise – an economic system not notorious for its conservative social effects.

It may be a bad argument, then, to suggest that an author or historical figure who believed in *A* cannot also have believed in *B*, and on the sole ground that *A* and *B* are incompatible. Very few mortals are consistent in their convictions, even at a given time; almost none, it seems likely, over a lifetime. It is a natural part of the human condition to believe in incompatibles.

5. A disjunction is false when it unreasonably requires us to reject all explanations but one: that because an event had one cause, for example, it cannot also have had another.

If the First World War was caused by German imperial ambitions, it might be suggested, then the Tsar's decision to mobilize cannot have caused it. But most human events have more than one cause. And false disjunctions can infect theoretical questions too: in *The Whig Interpretation of History* (1931), for example, Herbert Butterfield argued that since the past is richly complex, it cannot be right to see it (as the great Whig historians like Macaulay did) as a diagram of human liberty. But complexities can be represented diagrammatically, and it can be highly useful to do so: the London Underground, for example, is represented by one so simple that even ignorant travellers can find their way about in it; and it would not be sensible to object that the authors of that diagram were ignorant of the complexities of the Underground, or that they were seeking to misrepresent it, or that they have misrepresented it.

6. Some critical mistakes are mistakes of context and *genre*. It has been thought remarkable, for example, that Jane Austen does not mention the Napoleonic wars anywhere in her six novels – though no critic seems to think it remarkable if Iris Murdoch in her fiction does not mention Vietnam. Why should she? Social fiction is not required or even expected to mirror great public events, and it is not sensible to charge its authors with a remote indifference if they fail to do so.

7. Other mistakes relate to tone. It is sometimes suggested, for example, that a view cannot be seriously attributed to an author – courtly love, for example, to Andreas Capellanus in the twelfth century – if he can be shown to have treated it as a joke; or that Jane Austen cannot be a defender of conventional social views in her time because she makes fun of them.

But people often joke about their deepest convictions; Gibbon notoriously does so, for example, in the *Decline and Fall of the*

Roman Empire. So does Evelyn Waugh in his novels. Racialists make jokes about other races, and few would think that a reasonable ground for doubting the sincerity of their racial views. A work can be frivolous in tone and serious in content. Or vice versa.

8. Coincidences occur. It may be no more than a coincidence, for example, if Gilbert White of Selborne in his diary for January 1793 mentions the execution of the French king and the song of the thrush heralding the return of spring, and for no reason but that both events happened at the same time; and the elaborate notion that the passage proves White was recalling the traditional sense of 'revolution' as a seasonal return is too elaborate to be credited. Because John Milton believed in certain doctrines also entertained by Muggletonians, it does not follow that Milton was a Muggletonian, or that he was favourable to them – or even that he knew who they were or what they believed. Nor is a literary or intellectual influence established by showing that two authors inhabited the same town, or even the same street, at the same time; or that a young woman in London in the 1590s was the Dark Lady of Shakespeare's sonnets because her hair was brown.

9. A statement of intent, whether in the arts or in public affairs, is not necessarily to be believed, though it is always to be taken into account. Taking historical evidence into account is not the same as believing it. Authors sometimes misrepresent their intentions, and politicians are famous for doing so. It has usually been believed that Virgil wrote the *Aeneid* in praise of Augustus Caesar, and perhaps he did; but even if a preface had survived from his hand proclaiming that intention, it might not settle the matter, though it could not be ignored. (He had an interest, after all, in appearing to the Roman world as a supporter of the empire.) That interest, equally, would not prove that he was lying: in human motives, interest and conviction sometimes genuinely coincide. But authors, like other men, may easily be mistaken in describing their motives – or forgetful, or mendacious.

10. Some arguments are bad because of terminological confusion. A picaresque novel, for example, is a novel of which the hero is a *picarò* – a cunning rogue, or at least a scamp – and the word 'picaresque' is not a synonym for episodic. *Gil Blas* and *Tom Jones*, then, are novels in the picaresque tradition: *Don Quixote* and *Tristram Shandy*, episodic though they are, are not. On a

larger plane, 'scientific' is not a synonym for truth, since many assertions made by scientists since Aristotle have been false, and have been shown to be false, and are none the less scientific for that.

11. To know something is not, or not necessarily, to be able to give an account of it, in the sense of a sufficient and exclusive account like a verbal definition. The fact that we cannot define tragedy, then – in the sense that there is no definition agreed among critics about what is required of a theatrical work to call it that – is not a ground for concluding that we do not know what tragedy is. (It is consistent with that conclusion, doubtless, but does not require it.) Much, and perhaps most, of what we know we should fare as badly at defining, and yet we know it none the less. The demand for a definition, universally applied, is a philosophically ignorant demand, if it is meant to imply that only when it is satisfied can we reasonably claim to know at all.

12. A proposition is not reliably to be judged by the grounds that have caused some one to believe it. A ground for believing in a true proposition may have been highly inadequate, and the proposition no less true for that. My reasons, as a non-mathematician, for believing that $\pi = 3.14159$ etc. might well be called highly inadequate, since I cannot even follow the arguments that have led to that conclusion. That does not alter the fact that in any perfect circle the relation of circumference to diameter is rightly expressed by an irrational number of that order.

One way to describe my belief in π would be to say that I believe it on authority; another, that I have been conditioned into believing it. Neither description is inaccurate; though either of them, if left unexplained, might be thought designed to reduce the standing of π in the scholarly world. But what the instance really demonstrates, if soberly pondered, is that no proposition is any the worse for having been believed on inadequate grounds.

13. Things may exist even when they are unnamed, and even when they have no name. It is sometimes suggested, for example, that the Middle Ages did not have architects because they had no distinct term to describe them; or that a university does not study linguistics, sociology or American literature because it has no department within it that is officially so described. This has been called the 'No name, no thing' fallacy. But when a medieval artisan designed a Gothic cathedral, he was an architect,

whether there was a word for it or not; and one can very well study language or society without using such words as 'linguistics' or 'sociology' at all. The eighteenth-century Enlightenment did both.

14. A possibility or hypothesis, without benefit of further evidence, remains only that. It is all too easy to let it grow into a probability by your second paragraph, and into an easy assumption by your third. This is called the fallacy of the Galloping Hypothesis. But if a hypothesis is no more than that, it should not be allowed to gallop – or move at all – until some sufficient grounds have been produced for thinking it probable or certain.

PART TWO
The techniques

Let others creep by timid steps, and slow,
On plain Experience lay foundations low,
By common sense to common knowledge bred,
And last, to Nature's cause through Nature led.
All-seeing in thy mists, we want no guide,
Mother of Arrogance, and Source of Pride!
We nobly take the high Priori Road,
And reason downward, till we doubt of God.

Pope, Dunciad bk iv (1742)

If any man praised a book in his presence, he was sure to ask, 'Did you read it through?' If the answer was in the affirmative, he did not seem willing to believe it.

Arthur Murphy, Works of Samuel Johnson (1792)

There are no truisms in facts: there are no truths that may not be stated as truisms, . . . no truths which a sound judgement can be warranted in despising.

William Stubbs, Inaugural (1867)

CHAPTER ELEVEN
Questions of style

Language is not language unless it . . . conveys ideas to some other living, intelligent being – either man or brute – that can understand them.

We may speak to a dog or horse, but not to a stone. If we make pretence of doing so, we are in reality only talking to ourselves. The person or animal spoken to is half the battle – a half, moreover, which is essential to there being any battle at all. It takes two people to say a thing – a sayee as well as a sayer.

The one is as essential to any true saying as the other. *A* may have spoken; but if *B* has not heard, there has been nothing said, and he must speak again. True, the belief on *A*'s part that he had a *bona fide* sayee in *B* saves his speech *qua* him: but it has been barren, and left no fertile issue. It has failed to fulfil the conditions of true speech, which involve not only that *A* should speak, but also that *B* should hear.

Samuel Butler, 'Thought and language' (1890) in his *Humour of Homer* (1913)

I am going to translate a passage of good English into modern English of the worst sort.

Here is a well-known verse from Ecclesiastes:
I returned and saw under the sun that the race is not to the swift, nor the battle to the strong, neither yet bread to the wise, nor yet riches to men of understanding, nor yet favour to men of skill; but time and chance happeneth to them all.

Here it is in modern English:
Objective considerations of contemporary phenomena compel the conclusion that success or failure in competitive activities exhibits no tendency to be commensurate with innate capacity, but that a considerable element of the unpredictable must invariably be taken into account.

George Orwell, 'Politics and the English language' (1946), in his *Shooting an Elephant* (1950)

This thing here, which looks like a wooden club, is actually several
pieces of particular wood cunningly put together in a certain way so
that the whole thing is sprung, like a dance floor. It's for hitting
cricket balls with. If you get it right, the cricket ball will travel two
hundred yards in four seconds, and all you've done is give it a knock
like knocking the top off a bottle of stout, and it makes a noise like a
trout taking a fly.

What we're trying to do is to write cricket bats, so that when we
throw up an idea and give it a little knock, it might *travel* . . . This
isn't better because someone says it's better, or because there's a
conspiracy by the MCC to keep cudgels out of Lords. It's better
because it's better.

Tom Stoppard, *The Real Thing* (1982) II.v

Writing begins in freedom and ends in discipline: the self-
discipline of a style.

For all but a few rare spirits, style is hard-won – an ultimate effect
of revision and editing. Self-editing lies at the heart of style: you edit
yourself; and anything like an air of careless ease is unlikely to be
either careless or easy. It is far more probably deliberate and hard.

Because it is hard, leave it. Style is something that, in its final
form, can wait for revision. Since it is unattainable at first drafting,
the first draft may reasonably ignore it. It is simply unrealistic to
suppose it can be achieved at a single throw. But it can be achieved,
by progressive revision. And the ideal properties of a good style in
scholarly prose are not in doubt. It is clear without banality, and
rigorous (so far as possible) without needless technicality. It does not
confuse learning with longwindedness, or long words with intellectual sophistication. It is swift, unfussy and blunt. It can be read and
understood, and at a single reading, by some one outside the subject
altogether. That – to repeat – is the ideal, not the requirement.
Something less will do. But if it is much less, a thesis will strain the
patience of its first readers, and damage hopes of ever emerging from
typescript into print.

Scholarly style does not labour the obvious, or eschew it either.
'Truth should not be absolutely lost sight of,' Samuel Butler
remarked paradoxically, in his notebooks, 'but should not be talked
about.' Talked about at length, that is, when it is a truth already fully
familiar to learned opinion. Argument needs to be swift at the start,
resuming in plain terms what the world knows in order, the more
rapidly, to arrive at what it does not know. At that early point, one
cannot be too blunt, and it is a mistaken tactic to allude rather than

to state. Such allusions can arise out of a false hope of stylistic elegance. But they can all too easily mystify or infuriate rather than charm. Lytton Strachey, whose elegance of style is not in doubt, began the first of his *Eminent Victorians* (1918) with the blunt statement:

Henry Edward Manning was born in 1807 and died in 1892.

He did not continue in that vein, and his book would not have been worth reading if he had. But it was still a good way to start.

Self-editing is a matter of detail; and it concerns words, phrases and even punctuation. There are some expressions which, however forgivable in a first draft – and most things are forgivable there – have no business to survive into a second or beyond. They are not forbidden: merely better avoided – part of a grey list rather than of a black. Scholarly prose is not licensed to be worse than any other kind, and the clear expository arts of the journalist in a good daily or weekly paper can teach the thesis-author something in verve and freedom from jargon.

Words like *valid, meaningful, societal* and *structured*, for example, might have been invented to be avoided, unless by ironists. *Thus* is a deadening word in most prose, especially at the start of a sentence; and *Thus we see that* doubly so: it would kill any paragraph it headed, stone dead. *We* needs to be used only sparingly, if at all, and it should suggest a rare and exceptional emphasis; *I*, an even rarer emphasis. The tone to seek here is cool, explanatory and varied, but not neutral. Like the best traditions of Civil Service prose, the prose of good scholars allows for bright and shade, for ironic nuance and even dry wit. Though never rollicking, it can be funny. Macaulay's essays are a nineteenth-century instance; a twentieth-century would be the prose prefaces and other scholarly writings of A. E. Housman, the best of them collected in his *Selected Prose* (1961). Both books are almost timeless models for the scholarship of wit, and the wit of true scholarship.

Superfluous phrases may find their way into early drafts, but they have no business to survive revision: *as we shall see, as we have seen; before we consider Y, we must first consider X*. That is to hum and haw – and it is as exasperating in an author as in a platform-speaker. It is always superfluous, in this context, to say that you are about to say something, or that you have said it. The only business is to say it, and once is enough.

The active voice is usually brisker than the passive, which can be conveniently used, however, for an occasional evasion modestly suggestive of ignorance: *no source for this passage has been found.* Some terms in critical prose are misused almost as often as they are used: *refute* does not mean reject but disprove; and *jejune* does not mean immature but (literally or figuratively) arid, so that a jejune style is likely to be one drily deficient in colour and imagery. *That* is often to be preferred to *which*, as a conjunction, and those who are fond of this correction are known as 'which-hunters'.

The besetting sin of scholarly prose in our times has been its extravagant love of abstraction. That is the extreme aspect of a larger failing: an excessive love of nouns – not just in their frequency, but in their emphasis. The worst scholarly prose tends to pack most of its sense into nouns, and above all into polysyllabic abstractions. An over-nominal style often derives from nineteenth-century Germany by way of the United States, but even in outer space a sense of style surely needs to be maintained; and the astronaut who announces 'We have lift-off' when he means 'We have lifted off' is failing in a duty to the language. ('We come in peace for all mankind', however, once planted on the moon, is not a bad sentence).

The effects are all too easy to parody, but there are all too many real examples. Consider the following, from an art-historian:

> Images of full presence double as evocations of absence and aloneness; openness upon the here and now yields to the impression of a remote, already encapsulated world of the perfect tense. It implies a concern with the ontological categories and values embedded in the sensuous immediacy of the object-world, and with the spiritual life which that world acquires with its commerce with the human.

A muddle like that shows little sign of having anything to say; no sign whatever of being able to say it. It is gobble-de-gook – the academic version of George Orwell's Newspeak. And abstractions like 'openness' and 'immediacy' are not the end of an intellectual process, as the writer fondly imagines, but mere crutches to help him along the way to nowhere. Such prose could only have been made interesting by the use of special cases and striking illustrations. As it stands, it is vacant and dead.

Prose can look inert, too, when it consists of sentences of broadly similar length, especially when that length is over-long. Vary it. The shortest sentence in scholarly prose, practically speaking, is one of two words, like the last sentence here; and its effect is highly anti-soporific. All writers need to strive, in the first instance, to keep the reader awake; and the arts of language, like those of music or cooking, depend upon a variety of pace and tone. 'Many things difficult to design,' as Samuel Johnson once said, 'prove easy to performance.' If all sentences are of similar length, then the reader will begin to nod off; if all tend to abstraction, he may fall asleep; and if all are of monotonously similar syntactical shape – subject, verb, object, for example – he will unfailingly wish he were elsewhere. A short sentence can alert him. And a short sentence at the start, thrown challengingly down, can make him long to read on – especially if it seems provoking to the point of improbability. How, the reader may naturally ask himself, hooked by sudden curiosity, is he going to prove that?

Beginnings are even more important than endings, since the first sentence of a thesis is perhaps the only one that everyone who picks it up will certainly read. Long or short, it needs to seize on the central point of argument: not a marginal point; and not, unless you are highly skilled at stylistic decoration, a point outside the argument altogether. Never write an introduction, then; and if you find that in your first draft you have written one, cut it. Journalists, when they begin their careers, are often taught to put their main point first, leaving any qualifications, support-arguments and lesser matters till later. It is always the first sentence, after all, that persuades the reader to read on – or fails to persuade him. Admittedly the standards required of thesis-writers can be lower, in matters of style, than those required of journalists. But they are not bound to be low; and no one is required to accept, in what he writes, that a severely minimum requirement is enough.

A thesis can be the last writing in a lifetime that anyone is required to read. It has a captive audience – of perhaps no more than a single, weary examiner. But it is not too early to begin to learn the arts that will be needed after thesis-writing has been abandoned, and when books and articles are to be done. Weary as the examiner can be, he may grow even wearier; and he will always be grateful for a prose that wakes him up. As the American public-speaking slogan runs: 'If you don't strike oil in five minutes, stop boring.'

Good scholarly prose is efficiently specific. It hits the point – preferably the main point – in its opening sentence, and certainly in its opening paragraph, and unfolds it in lucid stages through the body of the work. An argument is an ordering principle, like a story; and like a story, it needs to be in the right order to be followed at all. Each part of the argument, as it evolves, can be seen to relate to the contention challengingly thrown down at the start; so that by the last page, if not earlier, it is clear how the parts cohere as a total argument. By then an assertion has been made, expounded and justified. It was neither self-evident nor foolish, at the start, but something between the two. 'John Dryden,' a student's thesis once boldly began, 'was not a great critic.' That sentence belongs to the middle ground that is neither entirely familiar nor entirely otherwise, and it has the high merit of initial brevity. Entirely familiar, it would be merely dull; entirely otherwise, outlandish.

A thesis is commonly part of a continuing debate. Others have had views of the matter, in all probability, and published them. But those views do not exist merely to be summarized, still less to be ignored, and a scholarly style is at once respectful and dissective: aware of the critical state of play, but not merely credulous of it. It notes the existence of learned opinion, to which it hopes to contribute. But it has its own place to stand, and one that is not another's: its own voice that quietly asks to be heard.

Self-editing, or revision, usually means both shortening and lengthening. It shortens sentences, paragraphs, and chapters or sections; and it lengthens the total debate by adding substantial afterthoughts. Afterthoughts are the rich bonus that all experienced writers cheerfully know they can expect. To write a first draft is to discover, even before one has begun to revise it, that matters half-forgotten can be raised to the surface of mind by the act of writing itself. To think only what you are conscious of having thought is commonly to think little. But to write is to discover, and soon, that other thoughts are there too. That is why the full intellectual process of writing a thesis only begins after one has begun to write it, and why it is usually a mistake to delay in writing it.

Shortening compensates for lengthening, more or less, and you learn from experience whether first drafts tend to be too short or too long. For many writers, sentences are commonly too long at first drafting; and the short sentences that can brilliantly vary the pace of good prose are usually, in the experience of many authors, achieved only in revision. Most paragraphs, too, are commonly too long in first draft. On that level, revision is an act of cutting. And to cut can mean either to omit or to dissever.

Omission means the deletion of words and phrases which, like *as we shall see*, plainly clog the flow of argument with superfluous matter. No reader of a thesis expects all the points that there are in an argument to be made at every point in that argument. It is superfluous, then, to remind him that this is so – even, as he may irritably think, insulting to his intelligence.

Dissevering a first draft is a process that every author of scholarly prose knows of by some name or other, and more usually by some simile or other. To some it is rather like slicing an apple or carving a chicken. Lawrence Durrell, who writes fiction in a similar way, has compared it to cutting a big round cheese with a sharp wire, as grocers used to do: big chunks quickly and carelessly drafted are divided and subdivided into ever smaller segments, whether as sentences, paragraphs or chapters. Commas become full stops or semi-colons; a long paragraph is turned into two or three; and section-divisions or subheadings are conveniently inserted.

The advantage to clarity can be enormous. Revision is rather like mapping a dark continent. Of course such divisions were always there, in some fashion. They were imposed from the start, in all probability, by the notes out of which the first draft emerged – notes that dictated the chief heads of the argument. But after revision, they are clearly there for the reader too. He can see them at a glance; and an initial list of headings, in a table of contents, will allow him to view the total shape of the argument as if from a mountain-top.

Punctuation

The tiniest revisions, and among the most telling, belong to the world of punctuation.

Since question-marks are seldom used in scholarly prose, and exclamation-marks never, it is tempting to see all punctuation in terms of full stops and commas. But prose can be highly soporific if it is composed of nothing else. It needs to be varied; and the best variants are colons, semi-colons and dashes.

The colon has two uses: the first, which has just been illustrated, is to precede an enumeration – here an enumeration of two; and the second and rarer usage is to divide an antithesis like 'Man proposes: God disposes'. The semi-colon is of intermediate weight as between a stop and a comma, and it has the sovereign advantage, to the reviser, that it can be added as an afterthought – even on the final typescript – by the single imposition of a pen-point above a comma. And the dash, equally, has two uses: it can be used in pairs instead of brackets, since brackets can easily look inelegant in formal prose; or it can be used dashingly, so to speak – to signal a careless ease, as here, towards the end of a sentence.

True, a thesis *can* be written with no points but stops and commas, and many theses have been so written. Sad to think of the chances they miss.

CHAPTER TWELVE

The art of quoting

Wordsworth, as soon as he heard a good thing, caught it up,
meditated upon it, and very soon reproduced it in his conversation and
writing. If De Quincey said, 'That is what I told you,' he replied,
'No: that is mine: mine, and not yours.'
    On the whole, we like the valor of it . . . It betrays the
consciousness that truth is the property of no individual but is the
treasure of all men.
                    Ralph Waldo Emerson, 'Quotation and originality' (1875)

'Mr President, give me leave to ask you a question I have sometimes
asked of aged persons, but never of any so aged or so learned as
yourself . . .
    ` 'Every studious man, in the course of a long and thoughtful life,
has had occasion to experience the special value of some axiom or
precept. Would you mind giving me the benefit of such a word of
advice? . . .'
    'I think, sir, since you care for the advice of an old man, sir, you
will find it a very good practice . . . always to verify your references.'
J. W. Burgon, 'Martin Joseph Routh', in his *Lives of Twelve Good Men*
                                                                    (1888)

Quotation is of two kinds, primary and secondary.
    Primary quotation is from the subject-matter of the thesis itself
– from Shakespeare, for example, if the thesis is on Shakespeare –
and it presents, on the whole, only technical problems. Secondary
quotation is from the writings of other critics and scholars, and it
is a more controversial matter. It confronts the student with large
issues of principle and procedure, that is to say, and needs to be
taken first.

SECONDARY QUOTATION

It is improbable – though it occasionally occurs – that a thesis should ever be written on a topic wholly unconsidered by another critic or scholar. Most thesis-topics are already much discussed; in fact their discussion can easily represent a chief motive for writing at all. Controversy stirs more controversy, in scholarship as in conversation, and there have been periods when few working historians could resist the temptation of offering a view about the rise of the gentry in seventeenth-century England or the true causes of the First World War.

That is where the dilemma of secondary quotation begins, and it is one not easily solved. To quote abundantly from the critics can leave little room for your own arguments; but if, on the contrary, you neglect them, you can be thought damagingly ignorant. The first course leads to tedium and triviality, the second to an air of naiveté. On reading Buckle's *History of Civilization in England* (1857), Lord Acton remarked acidly in a letter that Buckle had 'taken great pains to say things that have been said much better before in books he has not read' (30 March 1858). It is a charge to be earnestly avoided.

And yet the art of secondary quotation cannot always be satisfactorily solved by vague allusions to the state of opinion. Scholarship flourishes through high specificity, not through shadow-boxing; and yet too much specificity can bury an argument under a load of waste. This may be called the Great Dilemma of scholarly composition: to quote or not to quote.

The Great Dilemma, in practice, can in most instances only be solved by delicate compromises. Some secondary quotation may have to appear in your text – always briefly, and preferably near the start of the thesis, where the state of opinion is briskly sketched in. Some, again, may be indicated in notes, whether footnotes or endnotes; and others may be indicated by the bibliography of works consulted, at the end of the thesis, and only there. If the Great Dilemma looks pressing, in view of the mass of secondary quotation that needs to be indicated, then it may be solved not simply, but by distributing references in all of these three directions.

More importantly than that, the whole argument may need to be conducted *as if* the state of opinion were available to you, at least in outline. The Great Dilemma is to be solved, in the last resort, through that 'as if'. An ideal thesis or monograph is argued as if it were written by some one conversant with scholarly opinion.

Secondary quotation, if judicious, is one way of suggesting such acquaintance, but not the only way. The more important way to suggest it is by an argument that would only be possible at all if current controversies had been absorbed and understood.

Scholarly opinion means opinion in our times. Not much point in defending or refuting Maurice Morgann's view of Shakespeare's Falstaff, which first appeared in 1777, unless perhaps that view has been recently attacked or recently defended. Not much point in considering even a recent view, for that matter, if it has attained no prominence and stirred no debate. Secondary quotation needs to be about something recent and widely acknowledged. If it is neither, then it amounts to an Aunt Sally in debate, and it has little business to be there at all.

The claims of specificity remain paramount. A weak thesis is that, more often than not, less because it is wrong than because it is vague. And its vagueness may be nowhere more damaging than in its narrow range of secondary quotation. But to that problem, at least, there is a plain solution, and it represents no dilemma at all. That solution is to quote, and to name the author, book or article quoted, with its date of publication. From specificity of that sort, at least, scholarship never fails to profit: it is always better than unspecified allusions like *It has sometimes been suggested*. Such shadow-boxing phrases have no place at all in scholarly prose, unless supported by a reference.

Where specificity has been achieved, secondary quotation may become the motor that propels the vehicle of argument forward. A source is seldom wholly right or wholly wrong. To argue, then, is to show in what respect it was right, in what wrong, and why it was one or the other. Such contests can sharpen the surface of critical prose to a fine polemical edge. Duly quoted and referenced, the source proves that the argument is no mere vapour – that one is arguing for or against a view that has been responsibly held and perhaps widely accepted. And the reader may need just that assurance. Otherwise he may be all too inclined to yawn and murmur 'So what?'

Two conditions need to be observed here. One is that criticism should be impersonal: a criticism of what was written, not of its author. Scholarly debate rightly has its rules of courtesy, like private conversation or parliamentary debate, and it does not profit from sneers or abuse: the truth of the matter at issue is what counts here, not the folly or deceit of those who have allegedly failed to see it. The other condition is that the argument of an opponent must be fairly – which may mean fully – represented. And that, on sheerly practical grounds, is harder advice to take.

How is one to represent the argument of an adversary fairly and fully without over-burdening one's own text?

It is here that specific reference can solve two problems in one. It is not just that scholarship thrives on specificity; it is also that specificity helpfully refers the reader out of your text and into another. He cannot reasonably complain, then, if the whole of another's argument is not there. He has been told where, if so inclined, he may find it.

Some theses suggest a coyness about detail – a coyness hard to explain in intellectual terms, and even harder to justify. Its motives can be extra-scholarly: some students feel it would be presumptuous of them, as beginners, to disagree with an established authority, and that anyone in print is more or less that. But they are mistaken. In scholarship there are no authorities: merely books and articles that have held the field until something better arrives. That may be a disquieting reflection, at first. But the first glimmers of a research instinct arise from the discovery that not everything in print is true, and that even less of what is in print is adequate. No good reason to delay those first glimmers. The sooner the point is seized, the better. If one is to research at all, it is better to start early. And the simple truth is that some books and articles never deserved their reputations, even when they first appeared. If it is presumptuous to believe that, then it is not too soon to start presuming.

PRIMARY QUOTATION

A quotation is primary when it is taken from an author or source that is itself the subject of the thesis.

No one doubts that there must be such quotation: the only problem is how to set it out on the page. Here is some advice, then, about the presentation of primary sources.

By and large quotation should always be brief. Your reader can read too; a reference shows him where to turn, should he wish to do so; and it is only in the case of remote and inaccessible texts that quotations have any good cause to be long. The real motive for primary quotation is analytical: you quote in order to analyse what you have quoted. It can be indispensable to have such quotation within the argument, then, at the sharp end of analysis itself; but it seldom has any need to be more than a sentence or two long.

On the rare occasions when it needs to be long, it is best taken out of the flow of the text altogether and given a wider left-hand margin, or indented. Verse-quotations of more than a line in length are normally treated in that way; so is prose, when it is longer than a sentence or two. In such cases inverted commas should not be used, since the wide left-hand margin is enough of itself to indicate that the passage is a quotation. They may in any case be needed for quotations within quotations, as in dialogue.

References always need to be given, but as unfussily as possible, and they do not always require a footnote or an end-note. As seldom as possible, in fact. When the work is as familiar and available as a Shakespeare play or Milton's *Paradise Lost*, and when it exists (as they do) in many editions, such references are best given in a form that applies to all or most editions: act, scene and line for a Shakespeare quotation; book and lines for a Miltonic; and chapter-number for a famous and classic novel rather than a page-reference – such references being conveniently tucked into round brackets immediately after the quotation, to avoid the fuss of a separate note.

If the source has already been given in the argument, then it may be omitted from the end of the quotation altogether. This is called a buried reference. For example:

> And George Orwell ends *Animal Farm* (1945) with a sentence that reveals how deeply he feared that the two great systems of East and West – Communist and anti-Communist – might soon converge and become indistinguishable:
>> The creatures outside looked from pig to man, and from man to pig, and from pig to man again; but already it was impossible to say which was which.

Since the quotation has already been identified in the argument as the last sentence of the novel, there can be no further case for a reference of any sort.

FOOTNOTES

When references are fully given – usually in a footnote – they need to be in standard form.

That form is easily learned; and once learnt, it is a skill that lasts a lifetime. It consists of author and title separated by a comma, followed by the place and year of publication together and within round brackets. The name of the publisher is not usually thought necessary. Titles of books – that is, separate publications – are underlined, which to a printer would signify italics; titles of parts of books, such as articles or short poems, are not underlined but entered within single inverted commas, followed by the underlined title of the work in which they appear. That enables the reader to distinguish at a glance between books and parts of books – titles he can look for in a library catalogue, that is to say, and titles that he cannot. To take a poetical example:

> William Wordsworth, *The Prelude* (London, 1850) II.67–9.
> William Wordsworth, 'Tintern Abbey', in Wordsworth and Coleridge, *Lyrical Ballads* (Bristol and London, 1798) 11.8–9.

If the article is from a periodical, then the periodical title is underlined – followed by the volume-number (preferably in arabic) and the year of publication in brackets, and the pages. That is the normal usage for an annual or a quarterly – for example:

> Ross McKibbin, 'Why was there no Marxism in Great Britain?', *English Historical Review* 99 (1984).

A further refinement, as suggested here, is that the titles of separate publications should be capitalized, those of its parts – an article-title, for example – not.

If the periodical quoted is a daily, weekly or monthly, then it may be more convenient to enter a date rather than a volume-number. For example:

> Iain McGilchrist, 'Critical reflections', *TLS* (23 November 1984).

There is small point, or none, in using confusing abbreviations such as *ibid.* (in the same place), *op. cit.* (in the work already quoted) or *ed. cit.* (in the edition already quoted). The space they save is usually negligible, and an abbreviation has no reason to exist except in order to save space. Plainer to repeat the title of the work quoted, whether in full or (if it is long) in shorthand – for example, *Robinson Crusoe*. Abbreviations are in general to be sceptically regarded, and most theses are better without them. *TLS*, quoted above, is not an exception here. Though it was once an abbreviation, it is by now the real title of a well-known London literary weekly that began life in 1902 as the *Times Literary Supplement*.

It is only when abbreviations repeatedly save space that they earn their keep. A thesis on Milton, for example, might find it useful to refer to three of his best known poems as *PL, PR* and *SA*, in order to tuck such abbreviations, with line-references, immediately after verse-quotations. In that case all abbreviations must be explained in alphabetical order at the head of the thesis, most naturally after the preface, and in a column, e.g.

PL Paradise Lost
PR Paradise Regained
SA Samson Agonistes

The worst offence here, and one rightly seen as contemptuous of the reader and of all scholarly process, is inconsistency. Whatever is formally done must be consistently done. Anything less will look absurd even at first glance. If you sometimes give place of publication, for example, sometimes the name of the publisher, sometimes neither and sometimes both, then an entirely natural and profoundly damaging conclusion will be drawn.

And that conclusion will be that you are not even trying to get it right.

No element in a thesis is more susceptible to error than quotations and their references.

That is because they have often been conveyed across several stages of copy: from scribbled notes to first draft and so into later drafts. It would be surprising, then, if they did not need verifying at the last stage of a thesis, and before submitting it. Such verification, to be certain, needs to be made to the original source, whether in book, article or manuscript. If it is not made, then the thesis will look vulnerable at the very points where its weaknesses are most easily exposed. Many an examiner, that is, is capable of taking a thesis into a library and testing the accuracy of its quotations and their references for himself.

CHAPTER THIRTEEN
Editing a text

Since the landscape of eighteenth-century poetry is now apparently so
well mapped, and likely to afford so few unexpected perspectives, . . .
it will seem outrageous to suggest that we still know very little about
the subject.

Yet given the sheer quantity of verse published in the century, . . .
this must literally be the case. How confident can we be that
generations of historians and anthologists have efficiently sifted through
this rubble in search of anything of value? With some honourable
exceptions, they have in fact returned again and again to the same
familiar material . . .: explicable only if we recognize the hynotically
influential way in which the eighteenth century suceeded in
anthologizing itself . . .

In the decade of unprecedented social tension which followed the
French Revolution, it need be no surprise that moderation, decorum,
restraint and propriety were the criteria controlling admission . . . –
the very qualities which have helped to impart an air of remoteness
and insubstantiality to much eighteenth-century poetry. There could be
no place for the eccentric, the vulgar, the extravagant, the disturbing,
the subversive.

Roger Lonsdale, *New Oxford Book of Eighteenth-century Verse* (1984)

There is a feeling, often justified, that it is annoying when an author
writes his own notes, so I shall give a note about these notes.

It is impertinent to expect hard work from the reader merely
because you have failed to show what you were comparing to what;
and though to write notes on such a point is a confession of failure, it
seems an inoffensive one . . . There is no longer a reasonably small
field which may be taken as general knowledge. It is impertinent to
suggest that the reader ought to possess already any odd bit of
information one may have picked up in a field where one is oneself
ignorant; such a point may be explained in a note without trouble to

anybody; and it does not require much fortitude to endure seeing v
you already know in a note.

William Empson, *Poems* (1935)

Edit, indeed! Thank God they do. If it had not been for scholars
working themselves blind copying and collating manuscripts, how
many poems would be unavailable . . . and how many others full of
lines that made no sense?

Nor has the invention of printing made editors unnecessary. Lucky
the poet whose collected works are not full of misprints. Even a
young poet knows, or very soon will realise, that but for scholars he
would be at the mercy of the literary taste of a past generation, since
once a book has gone out of print and been forgotten only the scholar
with his unselfish courage to read the unreadable will retrieve the rare
prize.

W. H. Auden, *Making, Knowing and Judging* (1956)

Editing is easier than the world knows.

Most people imagine they could write a book – usually because
they confuse writing with having something to say. Few imagine
they could edit a text, at least to the point where it might be
seriously considered for publication. And they can be mistaken.
Scholarship, it has been said, though tedious, is easy: criticism,
though delightful, is difficult. The techniques of editing are none of
them beyond the average in intelligence, though they can demand
something well beyond the average in patience and persistence.

An edited text can make a magnificent thesis: original, surprising,
and useful to scholarship to a point where it may have to be
published. And since its introduction is a critical essay, editing does
not forbid the exercise of a critical sense. It might rather be said to
encourage, even require it. As matters stand in academic publishing,
an editor or publisher is far more likely to want an edition than a
critical monograph. A monograph may be of interest to the world
largely because its author is – so it can hardly be called an ideal form
for beginners. An edition, by contrast, can be of interest to the world
because of the intrinsic value of the text itself.

CHOOSING A TEXT

It is an illusion to suppose that the most important texts have been
edited already, still more of an illusion to suppose that they have

been edited in any adequate sense; and to search for a text on that crippling assumption is to condemn oneself in advance to triviality. There are great and totally unedited literary and historical texts. It is not essential, then, to seek out an unpublished manuscript – or even a printed work that has not been reprinted for centuries. Some of the most oft-reprinted texts are unedited, especially in the field of prose fiction. The Waverley novels are still largely unedited, for example, though Sir Walter Scott is not usually thought of as a minor novelist.

To edit is to establish a text and to write an introduction and a commentary. If a text has not received that threefold treatment, then it is unedited; if it has not received it sufficiently, and deserves more, then it is under-edited. Most novels of the past three centuries, then, are simply unedited; and it is only in the past half century, or little more, that the notion of editing the greatest of all modern literary forms has been mooted at all. The first to receive such scholarly attention in English was Jane Austen, who was edited by R. W. Chapman in 1923 and after; the pioneering Oxford English Novels series, which dealt mainly in short novels of the eighteenth and early nineteenth centuries, did not begin to appear till 1964; and the Clarendon edition of Charles Dickens, still incomplete, began to appear as late as 1966, with Kathleen Tillotson's monumental edition of *Oliver Twist*.

A novel is usually too long as a text to be considered for a thesis, even granting that the edited text itself is not usually counted as part of the word-limit. But some novels are very short, especially before 1800, as a glance at the 'Minor Fiction 1660–1800' section of the *New Cambridge Bibliography of English Literature* vol 2 (1971) will show; it is an annotated list that indicates which novels are unedited in modern terms – a vast majority – with useful notes on their form and style. Part of a novel, in any case, could represent the right length for a thesis, especially if it was extensively revised by its author: Henry James's *The American* (1877), for example, was richly revised by James for the New York edition of 1907–9, and there is a Scolar Press facsimile (1975) of his marked copy. A detailed comparison of his early and late styles based on a single chapter of that work could not fail, if perceptively executed, to inform critical opinion about the language of fiction in general and James's own evolution as a novelist in particular.

If novels mostly look too large, a short story can be just the right length to consider here. Since it is among the most neglected of all literary forms by historians and scholars, it represents no problem at all to find an unedited one, even among the greatest of fiction-writers. The short stories of Dickens, for example, are still substantially unedited; the techniques of the Clarendon Dickens could be applied to any one of them, and it could hardly fail to add to human knowledge if they were.

The vital principle of sampling is nowhere more potent than here. Any text, however vast, can be sampled. And any text, however vast in itself and however frequently edited – even Milton's *Paradise Lost* – can be shown to have been controversially handled by previous editors. The first book of *Paradise Lost* survives in manuscript, for example, edited in facsimile and transcript by Helen Darbishire (1931); it was written by an amanuensis and corrected by several hands at Milton's direction, and anyone interested in how editors use or misuse famous texts can turn from that book to a recent edition of the poem, such as the Longman Milton edited by John Carey and Alastair Fowler (1968), and consider at some vital point how well, or ill, the task has been done. One passage would do, as a sample.

Almost all public prose is unprovided for. Though the speeches of Burke and Gladstone have been edited, or at least published, so far as they survive, it has not occurred to anyone to edit a great political speech of this century – though some of Winston Churchill's speeches have found their way into print, whether in Hansard or as books. And yet political rhetoric is highly analysable in its content, vocabulary and syntax. Nor has any but the rarest of modern plays been edited – Colin Duckworth's English edition (1966) of the French text of Samuel Beckett's *Godot* is a notable exception – though it can be highly revealing to trace the evolution of a recent play through its textual changes in rehearsal and in print – some of them, as interviews may disclose, made by the playwright on the advice of producers and actors.

For Renaissance and Restoration drama, recent series like the Revels have begun to repair the omission whereby scarcely any English dramatist of the period apart from Shakespeare, Jonson and Congreve had been edited in modern terms. But they have only begun that inviting task, and are nowhere near completing it. Alfred Harbage's *Annals of English Drama 975–1700*, revised by Samuel Schoenbaum (1964) shows the scale of the enterprise, though a library catalogue would be needed to confirm that no modern edition exists.

Many famous writers have left behind them unedited and even uncollected articles, as recent periodical-bibliographies like the

Wellesley (p. 48 above) have shown. Even the most advanced scholars have seldom read them, and they may not even know of their existence. They would be grateful to be told.

MANUSCRIPTS

With unpublished manuscripts, the field in its nature is even wider.

The case for editing an unedited manuscript is persuasive only if it is of intrinsic interest. No one should feel he is driven to manuscripts, as an editor, because all the great printed texts are already edited, since nothing could be further from the truth. If you know of a manuscript that plainly deserves the attention of the scholarly world, then that is a topic. But it is its intrinsic interest, and not the fact that it is unpublished, that makes it worthy of attention.

Such a manuscript need not be of a work so far unknown: it may be an autograph manuscript of a work already famous and familiar. The autograph of Thomas Hardy's *Jude the Obscure* (1896), for example – his last novel – seems to be as obscure as its title suggests, though not totally unused by scholars, lying as it does in Cambridge, in a library where you would hardly expect it, that of the Fitzwilliam Museum. Still more surprisingly, the manuscripts of M. G. Lewis's Gothic novel *The Monk* (1796) and of Dickens's *Great Expectations* (1861) are at Wisbech in Cambridgeshire. When Trollope quarrelled with his friend Charles Reade over a play called *Shilly-Shally* that Reade had without permission made of his novel *Ralph the Heir* (1871), the play, though produced, was never printed; but it has survived as an unpublished manuscript in Princeton University Library, though the copy is not in Reade's hand.

It is to the unconsidered trifle, then, not to the great and famous collections, that attention should be addressed. Little point in asking for a Wordsworth manuscript at the Wordsworth Trust in his old home at Dove Cottage in Grasmere: everybody knows that is where Wordsworth manuscripts are to be found, and highly professional Wordsworth scholars are already editing them, as anyone would expect. But some unnoticed scraps of verse, or a bundle of letters in a college library or county archive, are another matter. If they signify, the world will want to know where they are, what they are, how they relate to other writings by the same author and, above all, what a reliable text would be.

THE TECHNIQUES

Since an edition consists of three elements – text, commentary and introduction – they may conveniently be considered severally in that order, an introduction being normally written after text and commentary are largely complete.

The text

Two large decisions need to be taken and justified here – openly justified, that is, and most conveniently in a textual note at the conclusion of the introduction and immediately before the text itself. One concerns the relative merits of original and modernized spelling; the other the choice of a copy-text, or the text (usually printed) that will form the basis of your edition.

The cult of original spelling grew powerful in late Victorian times, at least for medieval and early modern editing, and its heyday was the early twentieth century. R. B. McKerrow's five-volume edition of Thomas Nashe (1904–10), revised by F. P. Wilson in 1958, is one of the great monuments of that tradition, which was continued by Fredson Bowers in the United States in such large editions as his Thomas Dekker (1953–61). As a tradition of Renaissance editing, it met its match in Shakespeare, who left no autograph for his thirty-seven surviving plays and (what is more) small reason to suggest that he took any interest in the textual vagaries of such of his plays as were printed in quarto before his death in 1616.

An original-spelling edition of Shakespeare's plays, once considered as the ultimate goal of scholarship in the English literary Renaissance, is now widely seen as an impossibility; and recent editions like the Riverside Shakespeare (1974) of G. Blakemore Evans, or the Oxford Shakespeare of Stanley Wells, now embrace the modernizing principle as both scholarly and convenient. Given the cheerful chaos of a seventeenth-century printing house, it looks more than ever like a will-o'-the wisp to seek a norm of spelling for such a period; and it is likely enough that the revived vogue of modernized spelling will increasingly dominate scholarly editing in English for the rest of our days.

It is by now ever more widely recognized, in any case, that for many old texts an original-spelling edition can all too easily represent a facile excuse for an editor not to make up his mind. Modernization, for that reason, is less and less likely to be spurned as an easy option:

in fact it is a solution increasingly welcomed by scholarly as well as popular opinion. A textual note may draw brief attention to the orthographical vagaries of the original text, with a brisk defence of the decision to modernize and (if appropriate) an explanation of such exceptions as have been admitted. Such exceptions might include capitalization, for instance – especially in early eighteenth-century texts, where there may be some evidence that capitals were imposed by the author to signal a significant emphasis. If original spelling is adopted for a Renaissance text, it may still be sensible to impose the modern usage of u/v and i/j.

Copy-text is no less vexed a question than original spelling, and it has been unvexed only in recent years. It was once held that the editor's duty, where successive authorial revisions survive, was to choose the author's final intentions. W. W. Greg's classic paper of 1949, 'The rationale of copy-text', posthumously reprinted in his *Collected Papers* (1966), borrowed the term 'copy-text' from McKerrow's *Nashe*, accepting the view then prevalent in favour of old spelling, and concluding that it was often best to adopt a first printed edition as copy, feeding into it later revisions made or authorized by the author.

That was always a precarious place to stand, and it is no wonder if the question has not remained there. The outcome of Greg's principle could only be highly eclectic, for one thing; and though Greg was right to insist that an editor exists to make personal judgements, there is still a narrow limit to the judgements one wants to leave him to make. And for another, it is now accepted that not all authorial revisions are to be welcome, and that posterity has a duty to itself as well as to the ageing years of a poet, playwright or novelist. Wordsworth's late revision of the 1805 *Prelude* for a version of the poem published weeks after his death in 1850 has no pressing claim to our preference, since it is further than *1805* both from the autobiographical events it describes and from his genius as a poet. Henry James's early novels often went through three stages: a first edition, a corrected edition soon after, and (for most of his fiction) a radical revision or rewriting for the New York edition of 1907–9; and a recent editor, Leon Edel, has judiciously decided that the middle stage of the three – the early corrected edition, that is, rather than the careless first or the elaborate afterthoughts of 1907–9 – should rightly serve as copy-text for modern editions.

It is no longer possible, in fact, to believe either in original spelling or in the dogma of an author's final intentions, at least as universal principles. Where only one text survives, the editor may reasonably resolve to modernize it, correcting evident slips of the pen or misprints. Where more than one text survives from the author's hand or supervision, the editor is fully entitled to make a choice on grounds of intrinsic merit and interest – provided only that he openly justifies his decisions in an introduction.

The commentary

A commentary exists to record major textual problems – not modernizations, that is, or self-evident corrections – and to explain what an intelligent and literate reader might reasonably be expected to wish to have explained. It exists to predict questions, in fact, and then to answer them. For the purpose of a thesis-edition, which is always likely to be short, such a commentary may most conveniently be arranged as a single list, linked to the text by line-numbers (if the text is in verse), or to section-numbers or pages if in prose.

Brevity is nowhere more excellent than here; and most good commentaries, like good sauces, have been progressively reduced from a larger and less economical mass. They start long and end short. The supreme watchword here is economy. Explanations should not be admitted at all when they relate to names which, like Socrates or Oliver Cromwell, are likely to be known to almost any modestly informed reader and easily found in encyclopaedias even by the most ignorant. Nor should allusions, when they call for explanations, be explained one whit beyond the needs of the text itself. The reader of a textual commentary should always be assumed to be as intelligent and at least as learned as yourself.

The introduction

The final textual note apart, an introduction is normally a critical essay.

It is idle, for that reason, to complain that one would rather be a critic than an editor. To edit does not merely allow one to be a critic: it requires it. And since most of us write critical essays far more readily than critical books – the essay is the natural unit for historical or literary argument, after all, and the book a highly unnatural one – an editorial introduction can provide an even better platform to the aspiring critical mind than an attempt at a treatise.

Even an essay, however, is better in practical terms for being dissected into clearly discrete sections; and it is doubtful if it can even be written – let alone read and understood – unless its problems are posed and solved one at a time. Nothing should be allowed to envelop itself into one large sticky ball of prose. The questions need to be posed and answered one by one: who the author was, in the case where he is little known or simply unknown, and what in brief was his career; whether the work edited has ever been published before, and how accurately or inaccurately; and whether it has been discussed before in print, and to what effect. In short, the introduction needs to include a blunt account why the text has been edited at all, and in what sense the new edition claims to be a helpful contribution to human knowledge. The reader will only willingly read it at all if the argumentative narrative is as clear as that.

Reassuring to conclude that in such matters as editing, originality of style – as opposed to originality of content – is of no interest whatever, and indeed of less than none. It merely gets in the way.

CHAPTER FOURTEEN
Manuscripts and their uses

In the future, fewer of such archives will be exposed to the hazards of the auction room.

The British Records Association, the National Register of Archives, and similar bodies exist for the purpose of aiding owners embarrassed by family papers to place them on deposit in Record Offices, where they will be properly cared for and made available for scholarly consultation; many owners have shown great public spirit in making such deposits, and thereby accepting the financial sacrifices which this policy entails.

I need only instance the exceptionally important and valuable Fitzwilliam papers, deposited by the family in Sheffield City Libraries in 1949. But sufficient of such material passes through the dealers' hands to justify one comment. One should always buy, if possible, items which are entities and have some cohesion in themselves. It is deceptively easy to fritter away money on superficially attractive fragments of archives which, divorced from the main body of the collection, have little potentialities for research. One certainly cannot blame auctioneers for fulfilling their duty to their clients by seeking to make their property fetch as much money as possible; and if a collection of family papers is likely to sell better when broken up into a hundred lots, then the chances are that they will be catalogued thus for sale.

In nine cases out of ten, however, the results, from a historical standpoint, are to be deplored.

A. N. L. Munby, 'The acquisition of manuscripts by institutional libraries' (1960) in his *Essays and Papers* (1977)

A manuscript is of use only if it is near. The first step, then, is to discover what manuscripts of historical or literary interest are within easy distance. The second is to know what to ask for, of keepers and librarians, and how to ask for it.

A manuscript may be in public or private hands. If in public, it is always accessible in some sense, though the sense may be a highly qualified one. Some manuscripts, for example, have been placed in public collections subject to limitations of use – even quotation may be forbidden, for example – and a reader may be allowed to see them only if he signs an undertaking to abide by those limitations. But such restrictions are likely to apply only to the writings of authors who are living or recently dead, and manuscripts in public collections are still likely to be better research-game – to speak generally – than those in private hands. They are easier to learn of, easier to get at, and usually less restricted in use.

If a manuscript is in private hands, then it is as well to remember that no owner is under any legal obligation to make it available to anyone. Any written request made to him needs to be politely phrased, with a promise of eventual acknowledgement, and armed with sensible reasons why access might reasonably be allowed. There is no recourse, in law or otherwise, to a refusal to make private property available, and any such access needs to be gratefully acknowledged. Nor is it reasonable to demand a xerox, even if one agrees to pay for it. If a friend or relative has a manuscript of historical interest to which you already have access, however, or if you yourself have one, then private possession confers an advantage in your case, and it might be pointless not to exploit it.

It is inadvisable to misuse elementary terms when speaking or writing to a librarian – and still more so when writing about manuscripts in an account to be read by scholars. 'There is no manuscript of *Jane Eyre*,' writes the editor of the Pelican edition (1966) of Charlotte Brontë's novel, Q. D. Leavis, in the first sentence of her commentary, 'although there is a holograph in the British Museum.' But a holograph is a kind of manuscript: it is a manuscript (usually of a literary work), wholly in the hand of its author rather than of a copyist, and it can be used as an adjective as well. ('Is it holograph?' means 'Is it entirely in the author's own hand?') Possibly Q. D. Leavis meant to imply no more than that there are no surviving early drafts of Charlotte Brontë's famous novel. An autograph, again, does not principally mean a signature to a librarian, as it does to most mortals, but an entire work in the author's hand – whether book, letter, document or marginal note.

Inadvisable, equally, to visit a library known for its manuscripts without an elementary acquaintance with familiar works of reference that may readily be consulted before conversing with the keeper at all. Many famous libraries like the British Library in London, the Bodleian in Oxford and the University Library in Cambridge, as well as many individual Oxford and Cambridge colleges, have published lists of their manuscript holdings, though given the nature of the case they are often out of date. Ask for a copy in the library itself, however, and there is a strong probability that it will show one that has been interleaved and studded with handwritten notes on recent acquisitions – another good reason for starting with a library within easy distance.

For historical manuscripts, the reports of the Royal Commission on Historical Manuscripts have recently been indexed both for persons and for places; so that you can conveniently start with the place you are in. For medieval and early modern holdings in North America, there is a famous register: Seymour de Ricci's *Census of Medieval and Renaissance Manuscripts in the United States and Canada* (2 vols and supplement, 1935–62); and for post-medieval English literary manuscripts, Peter Beal's *Index of English Literary Manuscripts* (1980–), which will list locations of British and Irish writers, autograph and other, who flourished between 1450 and 1900, with notes on their later use and publication.

For English literature, the best scholarly sources beyond these are a series of uncollected articles by T. J. Brown entitled 'English literary autographs', with facsimiles, which began to appear in the periodical *Book Collector* in 1952; and Peter J. Croft's *Autograph Poetry in the English Language* (2 vols 1973). Neither may ever entirely replace W. W. Greg's *English Literary Autographs 1550–1650* (3 pts and supplements, 1923–32), which was abundantly enriched with facsimiles.

The survival of autograph manuscripts, as one might expect, rises sharply with the centuries. Croft's *Autograph Poetry* reports only five medieval English authors whose vernacular poetry has survived in that form, including Orm and Hoccleve; but Skelton, Wyatt, Sackville and Ralegh survive from the sixteenth century – Thomas Sackville (1536–1608) being perhaps the first to master the new and (to the modern eye) easier italic hand recently introduced into England from the Continent. Other early English poets survive little, or not at all, beyond prose documents, such as Spenser, Shakespeare, Drayton, Marvell and Vaughan: Chaucer too, if the Peterhouse manuscript of his prose *Equatorie of the Planetis* (1955) is, as its editor believed, in Chaucer's own hand, with his own corrections, and composed in about 1392. No verse survives in their hand. But Milton does; and Croft suggests that the famous Milton manuscript in Trinity College, Cambridge, which includes 'Comus', 'Lycidas' and the sonnets, of which there is a complete facsimile with transcript (1972), may be the first English poetic autograph to have been preserved from the start as a literary relic. That suggests how recent the cult of the literary autograph is. Only one Donne poem has so survived, 'A Letter to the Lady Carey and Mrs Essex Riche', now in the Bodleian and edited in facsimile by Helen Gardner (1972); and until 1966 no poetic autograph of John Dryden was known. That no part of any of Shakespeare's thirty-seven surviving plays should have been thought worth preserving in autograph is a striking fact – nor any play by Kyd, Greene, Jonson, Chapman, Dekker, Marston, Webster, Beaumont, Fletcher or Ford: no English play by a professional playwright, in fact, before the closing of the London theatres by the Puritans in 1642; though some academic plays written for college productions have survived in manuscript. The single surviving leaf of Marlowe's *Massacre at Paris* may not be autograph; the Ben Jonson autograph of his *Masque of Queens* is not of a play but of a masque; and the only remaining exception seems to be the 148 lines of *Sir Thomas More* in the British Library, which may well be a fragment in Shakespeare's hand, and Philip Massinger's *Believe as You List* in the same library, which failed on the stage.

By the later seventeenth century, the survival rate grows; but very little eighteenth-century fiction, as a proportion, remains to us in autograph, and it is only after 1800 that the trickle turns into a flood. By Victorian times, indeed, the scholar's dilemma is reversed, and instead of too little there is suddenly too much; and by the twentieth century, when the market value of autographs becomes widely appreciated, manuscripts survive in extravagant measure – though they are not always open to be read, even when they have been acquired by public collections.

To read a manuscript is a matter for patience, but rewarding patience. For the early modern period, where a crabbed secretary hand and the newer and clearer italic hand of the humanists overlap, the best guide is perhaps Giles Dawson and L. Kennedy-Skipton's *Elizabethan Handwriting 1500–1650* (1966). That takes the story of modern English down to the mid seventeenth century. For the last three centuries, a careful and affectionate amateurism can suffice – if it is patient enough to watch, listen and learn. A manuscript needs to be studied slowly, to master its individual oddities: partly to assure oneself that it is indeed what it claims to be, by comparing it with other instances of the same hand – whether in manuscript or facsimile – partly to decipher it the more efficiently, and partly to enable one to recognize further instances of the same hand some day on sight. The point has not escaped even the forger, and it is the task of the scholar to defeat forgers as well as inventors of careless attributions.

'By my life,' Malvolio fatefully remarks in *Twelfth Night*, when fooled by Maria's forgery, 'this is my lady's hand. These be her very C's, her U's, and her T's; and thus makes she her great P's' (II. 5). Those who paid millions for the Hitler diaries doubtless came to wish, as Malvolio did, that they had taken more initial trouble. Some even imagine that they can test character through handwriting: 'I want to see Mrs Jago's hand-writing,' Shenstone remarks in a letter, 'that I may judge of her temper' (July 1743). Such flights are better left to fun-fairs. When Jane Austen's Emma commends Frank Churchill's hand, George Knightley remarks that it is 'too small – wants strength', adding that it is 'like a woman's writing', though the ladies deny this. But it is not absurd to suppose that there may be gender-differences between hands, though they differ from age to age.

To memorize an author's hand can be useful, and it is best done by memorizing its peculiarities. Donne's hand, for example, has a high-shouldered ligature on 'of' and a low clock-wise foot to 'k', and anyone who has memorized both can dismiss other claimants with fair confidence. The other criterion is a general impression of the lie of a hand on the page: whether it is tight or loose, for example, in its use of spaces; though that test is unreliable in itself, if only because the size of the sheet may sometimes dictate the lie of its text. A third is spelling, especially in minor words like 'ys' and 'hys'; though not many English authors before the nineteenth century are constant in their usages, or care to be.

Hands are usually formed by the mid-twenties, but they can alter in later life – usually in the direction of growing more cursive and smaller. As in attributing paintings, unemphatic and less-than-fully conscious usages, like suffixes, can sometimes signify more than emphatic and highly conscious usages. Signatures, especially, can significantly alter down the years, and they can even provide useful evidence of a probable date where everything else is lacking as evidence. Dickens's letters, for example, when undated, have been speculatively dated in the Pilgrim edition (1965–) by noticing that the ornamental scroll under his signature grew longer and thicker as Dickens aged.

Authors make mistakes as well as copyists, and the fact that a reading is authorial does not guarantee its accuracy, when editing a text. The commonest mistakes can be *haplography*, when a letter, word or phrase is simplified by omission; and *dittography*, which is careless repetition.

Drafts can be speculatively dated or attributed on internal stylistic evidence as well as on handwriting. An idiom contravened, for example, or a stylistic awkwardness, or a reading that is obscure without a knowledge of the source from which it is derived, are all likely to imply a secondary hand – an imitator rather than the original itself. But such evidence is tentative rather than conclusive.

To read a manuscript, then, is a critical act, and one that takes something more than mere perseverance – though it undeniably takes that too. The critic's intelligence is likely to be fully stretched when he reads a manuscript, and those who mistakenly delegate such copying to paid or unpaid hands usually live to regret it. And to edit a manuscript is doubly a critical act. Many historians – including literary historians – never (it seems likely) use manuscripts at all. Some use them too briskly, taking notes of what they think they can use, and leaving them as hurriedly as they dare. They have failed to see the point of manuscripts, even when confronted with them. The task demands a different temperament from that, and a different tempo. It demands a critical awareness that not everything is of equal value, even if it is autograph and unpublished; that even authors can be wrong as well as right; and that the wise scholar is not to be hurried by another when he reads a manuscript, or even by himself.

CHAPTER FIFTEEN
Making a bibliography

Bibliography: the word has two main meanings, really quite different, despite the fact that they may shade into each other in some cases.

One (the more familiar to the general public) is a reading list, a guide for further study or a list of works which have been consulted by the author; and this will not normally give any detailed description of the books listed. The other, familiar to collectors, is a book about books as physical objects . . .

The kind which accounts for eighty per cent of the references in booksellers' catalogues is the author-bibliography: an account, whether in skeleton form or elaborate, of the printed works of a single author. This will normally be cited simply by the name of the bibliographer; so that the reader who finds attached to the description of a book by Donne the bare reference 'Keynes 27', to one by Gibbon 'Norton 12' or to one by Galsworthy 'Marrot, p. 63', may safely assume that these are the compilers of the standard bibliographies of those authors. He has, further, the right to assume that, unless anything is said to the contrary, the copy in question conforms exactly, in collation and all other material details (the binding excepted, if earlier than c.1830) to the description given in the bibliography cited.

John Carter, *ABC for Book-collectors* (1952)

A thesis best ends with a bibliography, or a record of works that have been significantly used to prepare it.

The bibliography is not a ritual dance performed to impress an examiner or to meet a formal requirement. It is an aid to your own work in the first instance; and beginning it early can help the labour itself to run the easier. Since it lists works that are in course of being used, it can help you to find them – especially if you equip its first draft with library press-marks to remind you where books are to be found. More than that, it can shorten references within the text of

95

the thesis: a book or article may be referred to all the more briefly if the thesis ends with a complete and exact account of its title and date. A bibliography exists in the first instance for its author, in fact; and to discover that is to make the act of composition itself the easier and the more congenial.

A bibliography lists the books and articles that have been used in a thesis, not those that might have been used. It makes no claim to completeness in general terms – only in terms of the thesis to which it is appended. Large bibliographies already exist on the shelves of any academic library to tell the whole story, and there is no need to repeat them – though there may be some point, where they are less than obvious, in listing them. No one will believe that a book or article has been used on evidence no more substantial than that it is mentioned in a final list. It is the argument of the thesis itself, and nothing more nor less than that, that will convince on that score.

If a book or an article is pointless for the purpose of the argument of the thesis, then that is an entirely sufficient reason for omitting it from the bibliography, however profoundly you may have studied it. Scholars who imagine that the dictates of objectivity require them never to heed their personal judgement forget that all scholarship requires judgement, and continuously so – including textual editing. A critic or editor who fails to respect his own opinion cannot reasonably hope for the esteem of others.

In the formal sense, a bibliography need not be a list at all, but may be set out as continuous prose, as at the end of each volume of the Oxford History of English Literature. Continuous prose can have the advantage of admitting critical comment helpfully and along with the entries themselves. If a formal list is preferred, then critical comments may still be added at the end of individual entries.

ORDER

If the bibliography is a formal list, then it may be marshalled in chronological or alphabetical order. Many thesis-bibliographies are less than a page long, and rightly so, and it may signify little which order is adopted, provided only it is rigorously applied. Never confuse alphabetical and chronological ordering. If a thesis concerns a single and celebrated author, it may be helpful to begin with editions of his works that have been *used* – and not, in any circumstances but the rarest, all the editions that there are – followed by a distinct and separately headed section of secondary materials, or writings about him. If manuscripts have been used, these should be separately listed at the start, with exact details of their locations and catalogue numbers. Acknowledgements of help, including access to manuscript and other material, are better placed at the end of the preface and at the head of the thesis than in the bibliography.

ENTRIES

Entries need to be reasonably full and utterly self-consistent in style. The best order for citing a book is

> Author's name, title (underlined) and (in brackets) place and year of publication,
> Author's name, 'title of article' (in single inverted commas), and for an article, periodical title (underlined), volume number or date and year.

In either case, the surname of an author is best given first, to bring it out to the left-hand margin. It is not usually necessary to give publishers' names at all unless some special emphasis is involved, and in that case they should be consistently given.

TITLES

Titles are of three kinds: books, articles and familiar descriptions.

A book title should be underlined; an article title placed within single inverted commas without underlining; and a familiar description like the Bible, Shakespeare's sonnets or Gray's Elegy should be left as it stands. The distinction between underlining (or italic type, if printed) and inverted commas signifies the difference between a title that may be found in a library catalogue under its title or author's name, and one that may not.

The style of entry may be shortened, for books, by a headnote to the bibliography in this form:

> *The place of publication is given, unless it is London, following the short title.*

That may avoid a lot of 'Londons'; and it makes the useful point that titles are not necessarily complete. 'Short title' is a technical term in bibliography to indicate just that: that subtitles may have been omitted, for example, if uninformative – or even parts of titles themselves where these are extravagantly long, as in the case of some eighteenth-century novels. Defoe's title for *Robinson Crusoe* in 1719 was sixty-eight words long: but who now would call it anything but *Robinson Crusoe*?

Example is easily better than precept: the best way to draw up a bibliography is to look at one, imitating its procedures in arrangement and punctuation to the last dot. Originality is of no interest in a matter which, by its very nature, is severely mechanical; and there can be a charm in knowing that invention, for once, is not required or even allowed. There is a brief bibliography at the end of this book, for example, entitled 'Notes for Further Reading', which can be used as a stylistic model as well as for information, though it does not represent the only way of solving the problem. It is laid out chiefly to inform. But it can be used, if desired, as a style-sheet.

CHAPTER SIXTEEN
Other theses, other books

> Learn as much by writing as by reading; be not content with the best
> book: seek sidelights from the others; have no favourites; keep men
> and things apart; guard against the prestige of great names; see that
> your judgements are your own, and do not shrink from disagreement;
> no trusting without testing; be more severe to ideas than to actions; do
> not overlook the strength of the bad cause or the weakness of the
> good; never be surprised by the crumbling of an idol or the disclosure
> of a skeleton; judge talent at its best and character at its worst; suspect
> power more than vice, and study problems in preference to periods.
>
> Lord Acton, *A Lecture on the Study of History* (1895)

Somewhere or other in the world, some one is writing your thesis
or your book.

Or rather, a thesis or book on your topic. For the simple and
encouraging truth is that no one in the world is writing what you
are writing, and no one could. Almost every sentence that is written,
and certainly every paragraph, is unique; and barring special cases
like plagiarism, it is likely to remain so. Unique here is not a term
of praise. Every individual on earth is unique, just as every human
utterance is, beyond the most elementary. There is no practical
danger, then, that anyone will write your thesis unknowingly, or
that you will write anyone else's.

It is easy, in such matters, to be over-concerned. But concern may
be rational when it applies to some highly specific undertaking – an
edited text, for example, with publication in view. In a case like that,
it can be entirely sensible to be concerned that some one else might
be at work on your text. And no published source will reliably
inform you of this: the Modern Languages Association of America,

for example, stopped publication of their 'Work in Progress' years ago. There is no way in practice of discovering the existence of a rival except through the grapevine of scholarly gossip.

Scholarly gossip is not hard to have, and sometimes hard to avoid. But then it is a question whether one should try to avoid it. It is highly educative. Where a project is as specific as the editing of a manuscript, then it is usually easy to learn of it through the library or private collector that possesses that manuscript. If it is an edition of a published text that is in question, then the matter is far less certain. But in ordinary circumstances, it does not matter if the topic you are working on is being worked on elsewhere. It does not even matter much if the other thesis is better than yours. They are not in competition: not, at least, unless and until they are offered for publication, and in the same place.

If materials are borrowed from another thesis, or from a printed source, then the debt needs to be candidly stated in the preface. Plagiarism is only that if it is unacknowledged. No thesis is supposed to be substantially original in all its features, or even in most of them. On the contrary, it can be a serious charge against it to say that it has failed to use existing and significant sources. Use here does not imply repetition of form or content. It is not a simple rendition that is in question, but an act of critical comment. Other critics and other historians may have been correct to have reached certain conclusions, and less correct in others; and the reasons why they were so can properly represent the chief matter of a thesis, and especially of its first chapter or section. Nothing is plagiarized when the debt is avowed; but equally, nothing is of interest when it merely repeats a known and familiar case. Scholarship thrives on the use of what other scholars have done. In fact almost any scholar would rather be attacked than ignored, though he might rather be praised than either. He wrote and published, after all, in order not to be ignored.

Unavowed debts, or plagiarism in the crucial sense of the term, represent the gravest charge that can be brought against a thesis, and one far graver than inaccuracy or ignorance. That remains true even when the plagiarism has been innocently or carelessly committed. And that is all too easily done, like inadvertent shoplifting. Careless researchers sometimes omit to record references in their notes, forget when they come to write that quotations are indeed that, and absorb them slipshod into the body of their own prose. The literary ethics of the late twentieth century are more rigorous than those of former ages in this regard, and rightly so. Debts need to be acknowledged, even when they are general debts that relate to ways of approaching a topic. That is the subject of my next chapter.

And when a debt is more specific than that, as in the use of whole sentences or even phrases, then quotation must be clearly marked by inverted commas or indentation, and a reference given.

CHAPTER SEVENTEEN
Acknowledgement

No man can properly be said to defraud another, nor ought to be so spoken of, who has not a fraudulent intention.

But it never yet has been proved, after all the pains that have been taken to this effect, that Mr Coleridge intended to deprive Schelling of any part of the honour that rightfully belongs to him; or that he has, by Mr Coleridge's means, been actually deprived of it, even for an hour. With regard to the first ground of accusation, it is doubtless to be regretted by every friend of the accused that he should have adopted so important a portion of the words and thoughts of Schelling without himself making those distinct and accurate references which he might have known would eventually be required, as surely as he succeeded in his attempt to recommend the metaphysical doctrines contained in them to the attention of students in this country . . .

He dispensed himself from it in the belief that the general declaration which he had made upon the subject was sufficient both for Schelling and for himself. This will be the more intelligible when it is borne in mind that, as all who knew his literary habits will believe, the passages from Schelling which he wove in his work were not transcribed for the occasion, but merely transferred from his note-book into the text – some of them, in all likelihood, not even from his note-book immediately, but from recollection of its contents.

It is most probable that he mistook some of these translated passages for compositions of his own; and quite improbable, as all who know his careless ways will agree, that he should have noted down accurately the particular works and portions of works from which they came.

Sara Coleridge, introduction to
S. T. Coleridge, Biographia Literaria (2nd edition 1847)

One sin of thesis-writing is ignorance. Its polar opposite is called plagiarism, where a thesis makes all too much use of a secondary source, and fails to acknowledge it. Scholarship lies somewhere between the two.

Acknowledgement is not as simple a matter as it sounds. After reading and listening, it is not always easy to unpick, even in one's own mind, an indebtedness to what has been read and heard. Coleridge is notorious for having scribbled things down in a long series of notebooks, often without references; so that by the time he came to write for publication, he had often forgotten what his source had been, or even if he had one at all. Innocent as that procedure was, to his own mind, it would rightly count as plagiarism in the stricter world of twentieth-century scholarship, and if detected it could be ruinous. Some examiners reserve the right to interview a candidate in cases where there is some reasonable suspicion, at least, of unacknowledged borrowing, to allow him to defend himself before a judgement is made.

The first protection, then, is to cite exact references for later use, even in the most private of private notes. That precludes the nuisance of losing a necessary page-number or chapter-number; and it effectively forestalls the ultimate disaster of forgetting that the passage was originally a borrowed one, and not one's own at all. Most plagiarism is a product of carelessness rather than of guile, but it is only little the better for that. A scholar is easier on himself if he learns to enter all references, and in the exact form that he will eventually use, into his own memoranda.

A bibliography to a thesis is usually a list of works used, but it is not of itself sufficient as an acknowledgement; and it remains inadequate even if the list is headed by a grateful remark of a general sort. Acknowledgement needs to be particular. The preface can be the best place to record large intellectual debts, whether to teachers or to published sources; and that record may be conveniently detached from the preface itself as an end-note, under the subheading 'Acknowledgements'. For the rest, indebtedness needs to be acknowledged in stages, where it can be, as an argument proceeds. And such acknowledgement needs to be precise, and precisely made at the point where it is due. It is not usually enough to speak generally of 'some critics' or 'some biographers'. A single name, at least, needs to be given, if only as representative; and if not in the text of the thesis itself, then at least in a note to that text.

There can be no good cause to prevaricate for long about one's sources. Friends and adversaries alike are a vital presence in a good argument. To quote what they have said or written is to propel an argument forward by agreement and disagreement, and most commonly and rewardingly by a critical mixture of the two. And when that procedure is as precise as it should be, it is not only the candour of the argument that profits from that precision, but its intellectual momentum too.

Where real scholarship is happening, the question of plagiarism, even of the most innocent complexion, does not even arise, since acknowledgements are made to sources at the exact points where they are commended or assailed. And no question of offence can reasonably arise, in either case. Many a scholar is offended, and justifiably so, by a failure to mention his name where some probable debt to his achievement is left only to be surmised. But very few resent attack in itself – for so long, that is, as it is candidly directed upon their arguments and in reasoned form, and not upon themselves.

CHAPTER EIGHTEEN
Teaching and being taught

Whatever is preached to us, and whatever we learn, we would still remember that it is man that gives and man that receives: a mortal hand that presents it to us, a mortal hand that accepts.

Montaigne, 'Apologie de Raymond Sebond', in his *Essais* (1580–8)

At school I enjoyed the inestimable advantage of a very sensible, though at the same time a very severe master.

He early moulded my taste to the preference of Demosthenes to Cicero, of Homer and Theocritus to Virgil, and again of Virgil to Ovid . . . At the same time that we were studying the Greek tragic poets, he made us read Shakespeare and Milton as lessons; and they were lessons, too, which required most time and trouble to bring up, so as to escape his censure. I learnt from him that poetry, even that of the loftiest and, seemingly, that of the wildest odes, had a logic of its own as severe as that of science; and more difficult, because more subtle, more complex, and dependent on more, and more fugitive, causes. In the truly great poets, he would say, there is a reason assignable, not only for every word, but for the position of every word . . .

In our own English compositions . . . he showed no mercy to phrase, metaphor or image unsupported by a sound sense, or where the same sense might have been conveyed with equal force and dignity in plainer words. Lute, harp and lyre, muse, muses and inspirations, Pegasus, Parnassus and Hippocrene were all an abomination to him. I can almost here him now, exclaiming, 'Harp? harp? lyre? Pen and ink, boy, you mean . . .'

Samuel Taylor Coleridge, *Biographia Literaria* (1817) ch. 1

A thesis often arises from a conversation with a teacher.

That is not usually because he has suggested a topic, in positive terms. He may even have discouraged attention to it. But discouragement can be encouraging too: to be told that a hypothesis is false, or that it cannot be justified by existing evidence, or that we simply do not know, can be highly encouraging, even if it is meant to be otherwise. If a view is unaccepted, then at least it is not trite; and if we do not know, then there can be a powerful reason for trying to find out.

To be taught, then, is to react; and reaction is a contrary motion. Some thinkers have even profited from reacting to their own earlier selves. 'What the author of the *Tractatus* did not understand . . .', Wittgenstein would remark, referring disparagingly in later life to his first philosophical book. What those who teach or write do not understand can prove, in the event, to be the motive force behind a thesis. Sometimes that misundertanding may reveal itself in nothing more than a silence, on their part: 'Why does nobody ever mention X?', one begins suspiciously to wonder. Sometimes it reveals itself in a mistaken emphasis in existing scholarship. The moment when that silence, or that mistake, is noticed is the moment of supreme enlightenment, to the intellectual toiler. It is at that point that a life of scholarship begins.

Irrelevant, then, to complain if a teacher is uncommunicative or unsympathetic. That, in a way, is what he is meant to be. If he accepts your conclusion from the start or (worse still) volunteers it himself, then the conclusion is unlikely to be of much interest. If he pretends to accept it, and in flattering terms – misled, perhaps, by the false doctrine that teaching should always be sympathetic – then he is failing to make clear what the objections of the scholarly world are likely to be. And by the time the thesis is written, it may be disastrously late to make that clear. A teacher or supervisor is an early-warning system: he warns you about what the scholarly world is likely to say, and what its most natural objections are likely to be.

There is nothing rewarding, by contrast, about agreement. Charles Darwin is said to have read for nothing but counter-instances or counter-arguments, taking note only of such passages in his reading that raised difficulties in the path of his own research. To understand that is to understand what research is. To be confirmed in what one believes could only be of modest contributory interest, after all, since one believes it already. Research looks not for cases but for counter-cases: it tests to destruction. If a teacher is unsympathetic, in that sense, then you are lucky. Research profits from unsympathy, especially at its earliest stage. It whets the appetite.

A conviction so mild that it allows itself to be dismayed by a sceptical remark is hardly a conviction, and the sooner it is dismissed the better. It was never likely to survive the long, hard haul of writing even the shortest thesis. It is the duty of a teacher, then, to express lack of sympathy, though in polite and reasoned tones. That is a delicate balance, and one difficult to achieve and maintain. But then teaching is difficult.

No supervisor is expected to write a thesis for his pupil – or even to show him how to write one, beyond offering general recommendations and particular warnings on first drafts. Responsibility for spelling and syntax belongs squarely to the candidate and to nobody else; though a supervisor who notices bad spelling may suitably recommend the use of a dictionary. Adulthood starts at eighteen, in the modern world, and the thesis is the work of an adult. As an adult, the student discusses early ideas and early drafts with a supervisor; and his object is to gain some sense, well in advance of the final draft, of what the world is likely to think of his idea and of his formulation of that idea. But the supervisor is not responsible for the final form that the thesis takes. It is not he who is being examined.

His advice, in fact, need not be taken at all; and whether it is taken or ignored – or, to speak more realistically, the extent to which it is taken or ignored – is in the end a matter solely for the candidate. No supervisor of spirit is likely to allow himself to be held responsible for a work he has not written. He recognizes that the student is a mature being who has the most perfect right in the world to reject his advice if he chooses to do so – whether politely or through silence. For another, he is rightly unimpressed by the complaint that he should have been more persuasive. No supervisor is required to persuade at length, or even attempt to do so.

A thesis-supervisor puts a view, considers the response to it, and answers. And that is all. Many a supervision properly ends on a friendly agreement to differ, and few outcomes could be more stimulating than such friendly disagreement. To disagree is to demonstrate that a point is something better than trite, and yet something too good to be dismissed out of hand.

Persuasion, in any case, is beside the point. Since the supervisor is not responsible for the final form a thesis may take, he is in no way responsible for determining that final form. His duty stops when he has advised and warned, and it need not be concerned with whether that advice or that warning has been heeded or not. Any author, what is more, knows that he can be persuaded without acting on that persuasion. Advice that one knows to be good can still be hard to take – in authorship as in morality. A supervisor, that is to say, like a publisher or editor, sometimes offers advice that a writer can instantly recognize to be good but which, with equal certitude, he knows he cannot take. It is good advice, but not for him. Nor need he be obstinate to react in that way. It is a matter of knowing oneself, and what one is capable of; and to ignore good advice can be an act of humility.

No teacher wants to be held responsible either for creating enthusiasm, or for knowing more than the student about the question to hand. The enthusiasm needs to be yours; even a touch of dogmatism, at this point, is not out of place. The thesis-writer believes he is on to something, and stands ready to defend his hunch against doubters, scoffers and other adversaries. He is not an ignoramus – at least not on the problem in question. Without that certainty, he is nowhere; and such certainty surely implies that he has taken the problem at least as far as its opening stage.

It makes no sense to say one is interested in a author, for example, if one has not yet read a single one of his works all the way through. Enthusiasm presupposes a degree of knowledge: the damage will be to yourself if you enter a topic in nothing better than a mildly experimental mood, hoping to find something along the way, or with an air of lightly feigned enthusiasm. It is you who will have to write the thesis; and to pretend an interest is to fool no one, in the end, but yourself.

Hoping to find something along the way is not enough. The fact is that something should have been found already, or at least glimpsed at from a distance; and the supervisor will want to know about it at the first meeting – even if it is no more than a hunch. He will also think it natural to expect you to have read the most famous book that there is on the topic, or at least to have read in it. A claim to conviction is meaningless unless that has already happened; a claim to enthusiasm merely vapid. And since conviction and enthusiasm may easily fade as you work, it is essential that both should stand high before you begin. Try to simulate them, and the only loser is you.

No supervisor by the end is required to know as much, in detail, about the topic as his pupil. A scholarly thesis can rapidly turn into a specialized enquiry, as it should; and it is natural that the teacher, after its opening stages, should know less about it than the writer himself. It is not a sensible charge against him, then, to complain that he knows less about the matter than you. That is how it should be. As it grows, a thesis rapidly educates its author to the point where he *should* know more about the matter – more, perhaps, than anyone there is. He should certainly think he does. That is of the nature of scholarship. It is not really difficult to be a world-expert on something, if the topic is narrowly defined.

The task of the teacher, when matters run as smoothly as that, is to know more than the pupil about the world in a general sense. That general understanding can warn and control, even as his particular understanding is outpaced (as it should be) by the thesis itself. Anyone can be an expert, if he chooses. The limits, after all, are there to be drawn by the expert himself and at will. But he can still learn from those who know less than he, and perhaps even because they know less than he. He can learn about how his thesis stands in relation to other matters and other minds.

CHAPTER NINETEEN
Classes and seminars

Socrates: But have you ever supposed that men who could not render, and exact, an account of opinions in discussion would ever know anything of the things that must be known?
Glaucon: *No* is surely the answer to that.
Socrates: This, then, at last, Glaucon, is the very law of dialectic – the strain it executes where, though it belongs to the intelligible, we may see an imitation in vision itself . . . When anyone through dialectic attempts through discourse of reason, and apart from all perceptions of sense, to find his way to the very essence of each thing, and does not desist till he apprehends by thought itself the nature of the good, he arrives at the limit of the intelligible . . .
. . . The older man will choose rather to imitate one who consents to examine truth dialectically than one who makes a jest and a sport of mere contradiction; and so he will himself become the more reasonable and the more moderate . . .   Plato, *Republic* VII 531 e–532b, 539c–d

One writes best alone, thinks best in company. At least most of us do.

It is essential, then, to attend a class or seminar – to talk about what you mean to write, and to hear others talk about what they are at. If no such class is offered, then start one – or something like one. It may amount to no more, in formal terms, than a conversation over coffee. But if that chance to talk is not there, problems will look bigger than they are, life will grow stale and sad, and no sense will ever be achieved of what is already familiar in argument and what is strange, paradoxical and in urgent need of explanation. Such talk may be formal or informal: but one way or another, it is inescapable. As God observed on creating Adam, it is not good to be alone; at least not always. And so He created Eve.

A class exists to promote and maintain a sense of proportion through the clash of opposing or corroborating views. It is not usually the best way to impart information in its wider complexities. For an adult, a book can do that better. Classes are for argument and counter-argument. They reveal there is more than one side to a question, even if convictions remain firmly fixed to the end. That is what they can distinctively do, and what cannot be done without them. If you are not there, you will not even know what other minds believe in the current of debate. And trying to write scholarly prose in that state of mind becomes a pointless activity. It is rather like trying to play ping-pong with yourself and wondering why the ball never comes back.

The best form for a thesis-writing class is usually the short paper followed by discussion. If the paper stretches much beyond twenty minutes, then the time for discussion is too meagre; so there may be some point in insisting that papers do not continue beyond that limit, and in interrupting if they do. A single argument can well be offered in a quarter of an hour or little more, and a single argument is what starts a discussion best.

A class is an opportunity to learn the arts of polite disagreement. Mere agreement, after all, is hardly worth having. One does not discuss what one has agreed about – or not for long. Impolite disagreement is useless in a contrary sense: it is the argument that needs to be attacked, not the arguer. Abuse is a sign of failure; it suggests that no counter-arguments can be offered. Some scholars, living alone or in the company only of admiring pupils, never learn to distinguish an argument from its author, and turn stridently time-wasting in consequence. But a class is always, ideally, a conversation among equals. No two participants are ever in practice equal, in knowledge or ability; but a class can train them in the courtesy of pretending that they are.

Not all students are aware, or sufficiently aware, that letters of recommendation can arise out of class performance. Applications for grants and posts, that is to say, may be supported by letters from instructors whose class or seminar one has attended. Since modesty, engaging as it is in anyone, is exceptionally engaging in the young, no one member of a class is usually required to speak up, at least at length; and there are commonly others present who are more than willing to fill any awkward silences there may be. But if one cannot be brilliant, one can always be attentive. Either way, attendance is easily better than absence. In some universities of the Western world, students will bombard a professor with requests to be admitted to his seminar, fired with the consciousness that it is their first step on the academic ladder. And they may, after all, be right.

CHAPTER TWENTY
Learning a language

All the little time I have away from painting goes into Greek . . .

I am almost thanking God that I was never educated, for it seems to me that 999 [out of 1,000] of those who are, expensively and laboriously, have lost all before they arrive at my age – and remain like Swift's Strulbruggs, cut-and-dry for life, making no use of their earlier-gained treasures: whereas I seem to be on the threshold of knowledge, and at least have a long way to the chilling certainty which most men methinks should have – that all labour for light is vain, and time thrown away.

Edward Lear, letter of 2 September 1859

Research can seldom be sustained by a single language, whether in science or in the arts. If your second language is weak, then you cannot start too early to strengthen it. And the earlier you start, the easier it will be.

A school or university is commonly a place where language-instruction can be had for nothing or for very little – whether in classes or by a computer-program. But it is astonishing how much of a language one can learn without the help of others. A smattering can be gained out of a book, and a smattering can easily be better than nothing.

It would be a mistake, then, to suppose that because one can never excel, one should never begin. Consider classical Greek: one can easily learn the Greek alphabet out of a book, and along with it some of the elements of Greek grammar. That would not enable you to read Homer or Aristotle in the original: but it would enable you to see which words on the left-hand side of a Loeb Classic edition of a Greek author are likely to correspond to those in the English translation on the right side, as well as to use a Greek-English dictionary like *Liddell & Scott* to explore the meanings and uses of a key word. It would also enable you forever after to read an English etymological dictionary more intelligently. And to stop there, after only a few hours of study, would be to find oneself better educated, in a vital sense, for the rest of a lifetime.

Advice to start a language only if you mean to go on with it, for these reasons, is bad advice: knowing a language is more like cooking or playing musical instruments. It is natural, for those who like languages or recipes, to be skilled at some and amateurish at others. There is no disgrace in knowing a lot of languages badly, or in playing a lot of musical instruments badly: unless, that is, one tries to perform in public. A linguistic smattering can be highly diverting and creative in its private uses.

Languages are ideally learned by children, which is how a mother-tongue is learned, and perfectly learned. That is the only language most people ever learn to speak perfectly. Anyone old enough to read a book called *Writing a Thesis*, then, is unlikely to be an ideal student of a language. But the problem, though ideally insoluble, can be met in practical terms. Perhaps the best technique, travel apart, is self-translation. Competence can be rapidly advanced without a teacher by mentally translating a stream of consciousness, or a radio talk or a film, or remarks you overhear in the street or on the bus. 'I wonder how you say that in French?' you ask yourself, and look it up in a dictionary at once, or as soon as you return home. Army cadets are encouraged to learn Morse Code in that way, to gain fluency, translating public signs into dots and dashes in their leisure moments; and it can work for the great literary languages too.

You learn a language, rather as you lose weight, by determining to do it. It is a state of mind. With self-determination it happens, even though it never happens altogether. No one ever gets to the end of a language – not even the end of his own. There is a summit that recedes, infinitely. None the less, one can climb happily upwards for the rest of a life.

CHAPTER TWENTY-ONE
Publishing

I have several times been compelled to refuse articles offered to me which seemed, from the evidence of the footnotes, to have been the product of real research, for no other reason than that, after several readings, I have completely failed to discover the point or points which the author was trying to make.

In one or two cases, this has perhaps been due to the author's inability to express himself in English at all. But in others the trouble has seemed to be rather due to a complete ignorance of the way in which he should present his material. Being himself fully cognizant of the point at issue and the way in which his research corrects or supplements views currently held on his subject, the author has apparently assumed that all would become clear to his readers by the mere recital of his investigations, without any commentary on the results as they appear to him. But such a mere recital of an investigation will only convey what is intended by the author to a person with the same knowledge and mental outlook as the author himself; and to anyone else may be almost meaningless . . .

If we analyse almost any piece of research which seems to us thoroughly workmanlike and satisfactory from all points of view, we shall almost always find that it falls into five parts, in the following order:
1. The introduction, in which the author briefly states the present position of research on his subject and the views currently held on it;
2. The proposal, in which he describes in outline what he hopes to prove;
3. The boost, in which he proceeds to magnify the importance of his discovery or argument . . .;
4. The demonstration, in which he sets forth his discovery or argument in an orderly fashion;
5. The conclusion, or crow, in which he summarizes what he claims to have shown, and points out how complete and unshakeable is his proof.

R. B. McKerrow, 'Form and matter in the publication of research',
Review of English Studies 16 (1940)

A thesis is normally read by a teacher or supervisor, in the first instance, and then by one or two examiners. Perhaps three people altogether, at most.

And that, for all the trouble you have taken, is not enough – or so you may anxiously or earnestly feel. It is entirely natural to think of publishing, even at the earliest stage, which is the stage where you are choosing a topic.

One may publish as an article or, more ambitiously, as a book.

ARTICLES

An article is not an essay, and the distinction is crucial.

In this day and age – however matters may have been in the times of Lamb and Hazlitt – there is almost no outlet for publishing essays. If an essay is what you have written, then, and you aspire to what is fittingly called the dignity of print, it will have to be turned into an article, and you will have to study what the differences are.

Essays are what Lamb, Hazlitt and De Quincey once wrote; articles are what nowadays appear in weekly papers and scholarly journals. The distinction is not solely a matter of documentation, though it is true that essays are normally undocumented and that articles can have footnotes – and sometimes must have them. The distinction runs wider than that: it is a matter of style as well as content. An essay is an expression of opinion, which is why – if you happen, for the moment, to be less famous than Katherine Whitehorn or Alistair Cooke – no one wants an essay from a beginner.

The differences can be usefully itemized. An article, unlike an essay, admits only sparingly (if at all) of the first person singular: *I, me* or *my*. An article is marshalled as an argument, with a minimum of digressions or none. An article is briskly phrased, and does not admit of flourishes or purple passages. And an article claims to tell the world something it does not know and needs to know – not to remind it of something it already knows, like Samuel Johnson's *Rambler*. An article, in a word, does not ramble.

If a thesis – or some part of it – can be converted into some businesslike form in these terms, then it may reasonably be offered to the editor of a journal.

The journal needs to be chosen with some care, and its choice may dictate the final form into which the article is cast. Since you have been working in the field for months, and perhaps longer, the titles of journals that publish materials of that sort are in all likelihood already familiar; and their addresses will be found inside. It is entirely sufficient to address your article, as a stranger, to a nameless editor, even if his name is known to you.

With that choice in mind, the length of the article needs to be within the bounds and limits of those that the journal already prints. So does the style and spelling, though American journals are well used to adjusting the national vagaries of British orthography and vice versa. Contributions must be typed; and since typescripts can be lost on the way, it is prudent to preserve a copy, whether carbon or xerox. Sheets should not be stapled, and typing should be double-spaced with adequate left-hand margins. Quotations and titles should be consistently handled. No bibliography should be appended, but intellectual debts should be clearly and briefly stated at appropriate points in the argument; and personal debts may be suitably acknowledged in a first footnote. Notes should be numbered from one to infinity through the article, and may be listed either as footnotes or on the last page of the typescript. The final page should repeat the name of the author, with his address, in case of loss of the accompanying letter; and that letter, which should be short, may be found the more impressive by an editor if headed with the name of a learned institution such as a college. No information about oneself need be given, at that point: the article is meant to stand on its own feet: to be worth printing, reading and consulting, that is, for its own sake. A stamped and self-addressed envelope should be enclosed.

Print is not the only form of publication. An article quarried out of a thesis-chapter, if it is of wide and current interest, may also make a radio-talk. In that case twenty minutes, or about 2,800 words, is the preferred length.

Weekly journals, like radio, commonly pay contributors; scholarly journals almost never do. For a beginner eager to place his foot on the first rung of authorship, it is a mistake to insist in either case.

BOOKS

Book-publishers do not usually count on publishing uncommissioned manuscripts of books, least of all of non-fictional books, though in practice they receive them in large numbers. Most monographs that are published, that is, arise either out of a commission or some other form of early encouragement. In the case of a scholarly treatise or monograph, the best way to introduce oneself as a total stranger to book-publishing is by a letter.

The letter should explain that you are proposing to write, or that you are in course of writing, a study of a certain subject, and it should be accompanied by a draft title and table of contents with an estimate of the total length of the book when completed. Estimates should be realistic, for everyone's sake. Monographs in our times often total between fifty and eighty thousand words, and it is unrealistic to mention a figure beyond a hundred thousand. In view of its printing costs, a publisher might find it as hard to publish such a book as you would find it laborious to write it.

A publisher, like an editor, should be chosen because he has already given evidence of being engaged in your field of study; and a visit to a general or a university bookshop will readily suggest what publishers are active in works of the sort you have in mind. A large and well-established publisher is more likely to be able to afford to take a chance on a newcomer than a small and precarious one, and there is no great advantage in seeking out a local firm merely because it is that. Big publishers can take bigger chances than small ones.

A letter to a publisher from a total stranger needs to be couched in brisk and practical terms. If it fails to give an outline of the proposed book, for example, or an estimate of its probable length, no publisher will think its author competent to produce a professional work. The letter should, what is more, clearly identify the kind of reader for whom the book is intended, and specify with exceptions or near-exceptions the sense in which such a book is lacking, and felt to be so. 'There is no study of . . .'

A near-exception is a book which, though close to the proposed, is inadequate for some reason: that it is old, that it is outdated – and for what reasons – or that, as well as outdated, it is out of print; that it is in a foreign language; that it is vitiated by a false general assumption, and why that assumption is false; or that it is unaware of some body of new material, whether published or in manuscript, which has only recently come to light. Publishers are understandably attracted by a claim to uniqueness, and understandably eager to test it by their own enquiries or by a visit to a library: 'There is no book in print in English on the Elizabethan love-sonnet,' a young academic once wrote to a London publisher who was a total stranger to him. There was, he went on to explain, such a book in French, and there had once been such a book in English, now out of print; and there were books in English on the sonnet in a sense wider than the Elizabethan love-sonnet. The claim seemed surprising, but on investigation it proved to be true. The publisher took his proposal, after some discussion, offered a contract and published the book.

For all practical purposes, a publisher, like a customer, is never wrong. No publisher, that is to say, and no editor, is ever under an obligation to accept anything he is offered by an author. His list is his business, and it is idle to pretend that he has a duty to think well of anything proposed to him. If he declines a good idea, that is his loss, and it is not for an author to complain.

But it is doubtful if good ideas are ever lost sight of in publishing on the whole – at least for long. Some authors have been known to collect their rejection-slips, which can be elegantly phrased documents, and to show them with pride: a more sensible reaction, at all events, than paranoia or resentment. An author, if he is any good, always has the last laugh. 'To write,' as Tom Stoppard once said, 'you need something to bite you.' And to have written, you need to believe you have written well. If you believe that, and rightly, you will be published – though perhaps not all at once. If you believe it, and wrongly, it still makes no sense of your motives to behave as if you believed anything less. And if you do not believe it at all, it is hard to see why you should have written. The faith and the heart and the love that it takes to write a book, or even a thesis, must come from you.

Notes for further reading

The place of publication is given, unless it is London, following the short title.

There are several handbooks of student writing, including David B. Pirie, *How to Write Critical Essays* (1985), which is designed mainly for upper school forms and undergraduates; and George Watson, *The Literary Thesis: a guide to research* (1970), which is for graduate students with a doctorate in view. Jacques Barzun and Henry F. Graff, *The Modern Researcher* (New York, 1957) is a lengthy survey of the prospects and perils of historical and literary research; R. D. Altick, *The Art of Literary Research* (New York, 1963) is a lighter account; while his *The Scholar Adventurers* (New York, 1950, corrected 1966) collects instances of literary discoveries. G. Kitson Clark, *Guide for Research Students Working on Historical Subjects* (Cambridge, 1958) is a succinct booklet for aspiring historians; and James Thorpe, *Literary Scholarship: a handbook for advanced students of English and American literature* (Boston, 1964) is designed for graduate schools in the United States. D. C. Allen, *The PhD in English and American Literature* (New York, 1968) is based on questionnaires.

On presentation, W. R. Parker, *The MLA Style Sheet* (New York, 1951 etc) is a minute account of American conventions; its British equivalent is the *MHRA Style Book* (Leeds, 1971 etc.) by A. S. Maney and R. L. Smallwood. Both have been revised.

The best introduction to the study of books as physical objects is John Carter, *ABC for Book-collectors* (1952, revised 1967), a witty guide in alphabetical order. R. B. McKerrow, *An Introduction to Bibliography for Literary Students* (Oxford, 1927, corrected 1928) is a longer and more advanced account, with highly useful appendices on abbreviations and contractions in early printed books, the Latinized versions of place-names and Elizabethan handwriting. *Art and Error: modern textual editing*, edited by Ronald Gottesman and Scott Bennett (Bloomington, 1970) collects classic papers by Housman, Greg, Bowers and others; see also James Thorpe, *Principles of Textual Criticism* (San Marino, 1972) and Philip Gaskell, *From Writer to Reader* (Oxford, 1978); or for ancient literatures, Paul Maas, *Textual Criticism* (Oxford, 1958) on manuscript transmission.

Writing a thesis

On books as a trade, Anthony Blond, *The Book Book* (1985) is a view from a publisher's window; and on preparing articles for learned journals, R. B. McKerrow, 'Form and matter in the publication of research', *Review of English Studies* 16 (1940), reprinted in George Watson, *The Literary Thesis* (1970), above.